12

GEORGE SAVAGE

GLASS

OCTOPUS OCTOPUS BOOKS

Acknowledgments

The illustrations are reproduced by courtesy of the Trustees and authorities of the following museums and institutions: British Museum, London, endpapers, figures 1, 4, 8, 11, 16, 19, 31, 36, 73, 78, 87, 90, 91, 100, 104, 116, 117, 124, 139; Château de Rohan, Strasbourg, figure 74; Kestner-Museum, Hanover, figures 50, 51, 53, 60, 63, 64, 67, 69-71, 103; London Museum, figures 101, 105, 108, 112, 113, 120; Percival David Foundation, London, figures 37, 41; Römisch-Germanisches Museum, Cologne, figure 12; Victoria and Albert Museum, London (Crown Copyright), figures 2, 3, 5-7, 9, 10, 13-15, 17, 18, 20-26, 29, 34, 38, 42, 44, 45, 47, 48, 52, 54, 55, 57, 59, 66, 68, 72, 75-77, 79-82, 84-86, 89, 92-99, 102, 106, 107, 109-111, 114, 115, 118, 119, 121, 122, 125-138, 140; Wallace Collection, London (Crown Copyright), figures 30, 32, 35, 39, 40, 49, 61, 88; Messrs. Christie, Manson and Woods, London, figures 27, 28, 33, 43, 46, 56, 58; Messrs. Sotheby and Co, London, figures 62, 65, 83.

Figure 123 is reproduced by gracious permission of Her Majesty the Queen.

Specially commissioned photographs were taken by Wilfrid Walter.

Preceding page
A rare small mosaic of Pompeian type made from glass *tesserae* embedded in cement (*opus sectile*). First century AD

This edition first published 1972 by
OCTOPUS BOOKS LIMITED
59 Grosvenor Street, London W.1

ISBN 7064 0038 0

Contents

1 The Portland Vase

Ancient glass

THE TERM 'GLASS' is used to denote a variety of substances made from differing materials. Glass is both hard and brittle, and usually it is either transparent or translucent, but not invariably so. It may be artificial (that is, made by man), but such volcanic substances as obsidian are natural glasses, and all have one property in common: the ultimate structure is amorphous and not crystalline, although in certain circumstances a crystalline structure may develop which is referred to as devitrification.

Glasses belong to a group of substances with unique properties which are termed supercooled liquids, that is liquids which have passed into a rigid state without undergoing any noticeable structural change. Glass has, in fact, been well described as a congealed solution of a number of substances, of which silica and alkali are invariables.

The temperature range necessary for the fusion of the ingredients of man-made glass normally has its extreme upper limit in the region of 1600° C, necessary to make a special glass composed of silica only. The actual temperature at which fusion takes place is governed by the amount of alkali present, since this acts as a flux which promotes the melting of the remaining ingredients. Other fluxes, such as lead, are described later.

The principal source of silica is sand, although certain kinds of rock are sometimes used. For the finest glass a sand which is virtually free from iron is essential, since iron occurring as an impurity discolours the finished product and is, in fact, the cause of the distinctive appearance of much old glass.

In former times the alkalis were derived from wood-ash (potash-glass) or by burning sea-weed (soda-glass). Wood-ash yields potassium carbonate ('pearl-ash'), and glass made with it is hard and brilliant, passing rapidly from the liquid to the solid state. Soda-glass remains in a plastic state over a wider temperature range, and is therefore more easily worked. Essentially, the former has been manufactured inland and the latter mainly along the coasts, especially of the Mediterranean, and identification of the metal is one way of deciding where an ancient specimen came from originally, wherever it may be found subsequently.

Lead is also introduced into certain types of glass. It was, perhaps, used as a flux for pottery glazes by the Assyrians in the first millennium BC, and it was employed in Chinese and Near Eastern pottery glazes before its introduction into glass proper. Glass heavily fluxed with lead ('lead' or 'flint' glass) is particularly notable for its property of refracting light, especially when ground into light-reflecting facets which characterize the variety known commonly as cut-glass.

The ways in which glass is formed and decorated will be described in their place, but it is essential to say at this point that formation nearly always takes place when the material is at a stage where it has the consistency of treacle, and it behaves in much the same way.

The origin of glass is unknown. Pliny (*Natural History*) is the source of the story of Syrian merchants who built their camp-fire on the seashore on blocks of natron (a kind of sodium carbonate) and were astonished to see rivulets of glass flowing from the bottom. This is certainly fable, and the 'camp-fire' theory is popularly invoked to account for all kinds of technical innovations, from copper-smelting to pottery-making. The fact remains that a camp-fire rarely exceeds 600° C by more than a few degrees, which is much too low for any of these purposes, all of which require a minimum temperature in the region of 950°.

Glass of a sort was known to the Egyptians in predynastic times, although only in the form of a glaze for stone-beads. These were the product of quartz pebbles being brought into contact with an alkaline flux in the form of wood-ash, and they were probably a by-product of pottery manufacture. Surviving pottery suggests that the necessary temperatures were attainable at the time in some form of kiln.

Perhaps the most likely explanation of the origin of Egyptian glass is to be sought in the so-called 'faience'. This was formed from finely-powdered quartz made into a workable paste, apparently with a solution of sodium carbonate. After a light firing at about 900° C, the surface changed into a glass-like layer, and this effect probably suggested further experiments which eventually resulted in the production of small and primitive glass vessels.

The exact method employed to form some of the earliest small vases is still controversial. It is probable that they were made by dipping or rolling a clay or sand core (sometimes covered with a textile to aid extraction) in molten

2 *Oenochoe* in blue glass with 'combed' contrasting decoration. Like the pottery version, the trefoil lip is made by pinching the circular rim. Egypt. Fifth century BC

or softened glass, the exterior perhaps worked into shape with wooden tools. Later softened 'rods' or 'canes' of glass were wound round a core, and decoration was contrived by mingling canes of coloured glass. Sir Leonard Woolley has suggested that this method was not Egyptian in origin at all, but a technique derived from Syria, where glass was probably being made by 1700 B C. This is to some extent confirmed by the sudden appearance of work of an advanced kind in Egypt during the XVIIIth dynasty (c. 1450 B C).

The canes were first wound round the core into the approximate shape of the vase, so that the interior was cylindrical. The mass was then reheated to fuse the canes together. While the surface was still soft it was often 'dragged' or 'combed' to produce a wavy pattern [figure 2], which to judge from the number of surviving specimens, was much admired. Glass canes of different colours were bundled together and fused, and then, while still soft, were drawn out and cut off into desired lengths. This innovation in glass-making was still popular in Europe as late as the nineteenth century, when it was used for the making of *millefiore* paper-weights and similar decorative items.

Another technique, which may have been Syrian in origin, was the fusing of powdered glass which had been packed into moulds of fire-clay. This primitive method eventually gave place to blowing into moulds for quantity production, and finally into glass-blowing proper, a process described later.

The early Egyptian glass-makers slowly learned how to select the best kinds of silica and the most efficient fluxes. Generally, silica was used in the form of quartz sand, pebbles, or flint ground to small particles. They learned also to colour their glass with copper, which yields a bluish-green colour under normal conditions, and to this extent copper-smelting played a part in the development of the industry, the pigment being derived from the copper ores of the Sinai peninsula. Apart from its appearance as a glaze on a base of stone or faience, glass does not certainly appear in Egypt until about 1600 B C with the expulsion of the Hyksos kings and the beginning of the New Kingdom. An undoubted example of true glass occurs during the reign of Amenhotep I of the XVIIIth dynasty (about 1550 B C), and very soon afterwards a fairly wide range of simple colours may be observed: blues, greens, orange, white, black, violet, and (somewhat later) red.

Copper was the colouring agent for the greens and bluish-greens, but, in certain circumstances (when glass containing copper was cooled in the presence of an excess of carbon monoxide), a ruby red was attained: a 'reduced' copper colour similar to those to be observed later on Chinese porcelain and stoneware. Black was probably derived from iron, or iron and manganese combined, although silver in a finely divided state yields black if it is included in the substance of the glass. As a surface application it appears as a yellow stain.

Antimony, imported by the Egyptians from Assyrian sources, produces an opaque white if added in fairly massive quantities, and although the same result may be obtained with more economy by adding tin oxide, this scarce metal was probably reserved for the bronze-makers. The Romans also used antimony for this purpose, the substance serving to produce the white layer of the 'Portland' vase [figure 1], even though they had ample supplies of tin in a suitable form. It seems likely that tin oxide was not used by glass-makers to obtain an opaque white, apart from Assyrian pottery glazes of the first millennium BC, until its introduction into Persian pottery glazes in the ninth century AD.

Violet, purple, or brown were the product of using manganese in fairly large quantities. In small amounts manganese acts as a decolourizer, neutralizing the slight greenish or yellowish tinge which arises from impurities in the materials. Blue was obtained from cobalt oxide, but the source of yellow is less easy to decide. It was probably derived from antimoniate of lead (Naples yellow), used in Assyria to colour the well-known brick reliefs. All these substances have been used to colour glass and pottery glazes ever since.

Engraving with hand-tools, cutting patterns into the surface with the aid of abrasives such as jewel-dust and the emery of Naxos, was also a comparatively early development. The Egyptians were adept in the use of abrasives, employing them to shape sculpture and vases in such relatively hard stones as granite and basalt. From a technical viewpoint, therefore, glass-engraving of a simple kind was not a very big step.

There is an essential difference between the techniques of the glass-engraver and the cameo-cutter (whose art developed from the cutting of cylinder-seals in Mesopotamia) which it would be as well to define here. Cameo-cut-

3 Small Syrian vase decorated with simple wheel-engraving. Third century AD

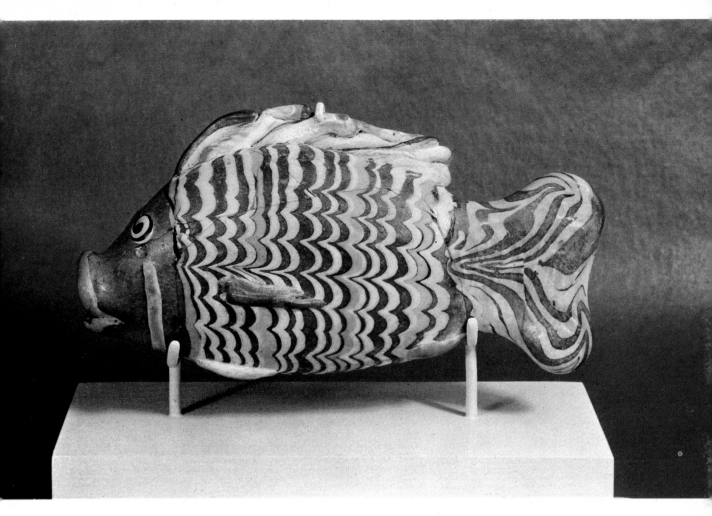

4 Fish of sand-core glass with 'combed' decoration. Egypt. Eighteenth dynasty

ters used graving-tools held in the hand, which were either diamond-pointed or charged with abrasive. The engraver's wheel (made of copper charged with abrasive, or of an abrasive stone) was rotated in a fixed position, the work being brought to it and moved appropriately. The first glass-engraving was indistinguishable from cameo-cutting in the technique adopted, but the rotating engraving-wheel was known in Pliny's day. In Book XXXVI (Chapter 66) he says, 'glass is either blown into various forms, turned in a lathe, or engraved like silver'. The reference to 'turning' in a lathe obviously refers to some kind of mechanically driven engraving-wheel, perhaps similar in principle to the pole-lathe, and engraving 'like silver' no doubt means something of the nature of cameo-cutting. Grindstones driven by a foot-treadle appear in Pompeian wall paintings. Simple wheel-engraving is to be seen in figure 3.

From the end of the XVIIIth dynasty until the period of the Saïte kings in the seventh century few glass vessels were made in Egypt, but the industry was then revived and manufacture was gradually concentrated in Alexandria, where decorative glass of high quality was made in many styles and techniques, especially those based on coloured glass canes in a variety of forms [figures 5 and 6].

It was at Alexandria that 'cased', 'flashed', or 'overlay' glass was first made. A vessel of one colour was dipped into molten glass of another, producing two differently coloured layers. Such vessels were then carved by lapidaries, who cut patterns and designs through the first layer down to the second, revealing it more or less. It demanded considerable technical skill to make the vessel in the first place. Glass contracts slightly as it cools, and the rate of contraction has to be the same in both layers; otherwise one layer will either separate from the other, or the top layer will break up into a network of fine cracks of the kind sometimes to be seen in pottery glazes when there has been a disagreement between the contraction rate of body and glaze.

Glass-blowing, at first rarely used in Alexandria, appears to have been devised in Syria sometime during the first century BC, where the soda-glass of that region was especially suitable for the purpose. This soon became the preferred way of forming glass vessels for most purposes, although it was at first limited to simple blowing into moulds. The operation of 'blowing' glass is effected with the aid of a hollow pipe while the 'metal' – the manufacturer's term for glass – has the consistency of treacle. The semi-molten glass is gathered on to the end of the pipe, which has a mouthpiece at one end and varies in shape at the lower end according to the class of object to be made. By alternately blowing to form a bubble of glass and swinging the bubble on the end of the pipe, or by rolling it on a table called a 'marver', the workman forms the shape of the vessel, which is then detached from the pipe. All kinds of additions may be made to a blown vessel. Trailed glass decoration, or such necessary parts as the stem and foot of a wine-glass, are fixed by welding. In its softened state the glass bubble may be cut with shears, or reshaped with a variety of hand-tools.

Blown glass is much thinner than glass formed in any other way, and the forms are characteristically symmetrical, despite any subsequent manipulation. Examples of blowing into moulds in ancient times are common [figure 17], and the most common are probably the Syrian bottles formed of two opposing human masks surmounted

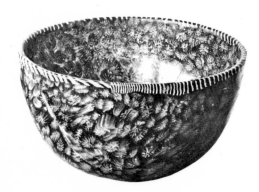

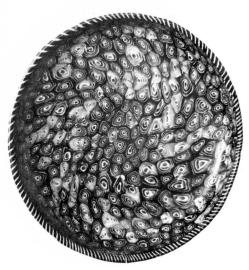

5 and 6 Bowl of *millefiore* glass. The method of manufacture from sections of coloured canes may be seen clearly. Alexandrian. First century AD

by a neck, on which the mould seams can often be traced.

The manufacture of glass in Syria may have existed before 1700 BC, and the distribution of Syrian work by sea (and Egyptian glass also) was no doubt later in the hands of the Phoenicians, the great trading nation of the ancient world, who spread manufactured products far and wide, even to England, where they traded for Cornish tin. It has been said that the Phoenician craftsmen did not make glass, seemingly because their reputation as traders appears to preclude it. However, their skill as bronzesmiths, evident in the part they played in the furnishing of Solomon's Temple, suggests that they were a technically skilled people as well as merchants, and that glass-making was well within their capacity.

By the sixth century BC Syrian vessels excelled those of Egypt in size, if not always in the quality of the metal, and they employed the coloured cane technique extensively. It has been suggested that powdered glass was mixed with a binding material and shaped either by hand or with the aid of the potter's wheel. But this cannot be satisfactorily proved.

Glass-blowing was probably first attempted in the Phoenician trading city of Sidon, and the kind of moulds already in use to contain glass-paste were adapted to the new technique, blowing without moulds coming a little later. The soda-glass of the region readily lent itself to a decoration of trailed glass threads, a technique later taken up in a similar metal by the great glass-houses of Venice.

Much of the Sidonian glass now existing may fairly be described as commercial, and from the large amount surviving, and its wide distribution, it was a popular article of trade. Much of it is commonly but erroneously classified as 'Roman' glass, and the Sidonian glass-houses provided much of the glass-ware used in the Imperial city, as well as some of the workers for Italian manufactories. In quality it never excelled the best Roman work.

Frederic Neuberg (*Ancient Glass*) discusses at length the many surviving references to Jewish glass-making, and the art appears to have been well developed among the Jews. Excellent sources of raw materials existed at several places in Palestine and Syria, and after the Diaspora, which had been completed before the middle of the second century AD, the Jews helped to establish the art at Byzantium. Nevertheless, early Jewish glass is difficult to separate from Syrian. Vessels decorated with such characteristic *motifs* as the seven-branched candelabrum of the Temple

7 Beaker of amber-coloured glass blown into a mould. The ancestor of the 'claw-beaker' [figure 19]. Perhaps Syrian. First to second century AD

11

9 *Tazza* of *millefiore* glass. Probably Alexandrian. First century AD

can be accepted without difficulty, and Neuberg credibly suggests that 'gold sandwich' glass [figure 8] may have been Jewish in origin. This persistent type was undoubtedly made by Jewish craftsmen in Byzantium. Gold-leaf was attached to the surface of a vessel and engraved, after which it was flashed with a protective layer of clear glass.

The Roman glass industry began as an offshoot of that of Syria on the one hand, and of Alexandria on the other. It can be divided approximately into decorative and commercial, the latter category being represented by the typical square bottles [figure 10] commonly recovered, which were made by blowing into moulds. The form was obviously devised for easy transport and storage. The Romans were not, at first, makers of the finer kinds of decorative glass. Their peculiar genius lay in the establishment of factories for quantity production, and trade-names of the kind familiar on Roman pottery and domestic

8 *(left)* Bowl of 'gold sandwich' glass. Syrian. Second to third century AD

bronzeware appear also on glass. This section of the industry owed much to the commercial production of Sidon, and of Syria generally, where the practice of trademarking already existed.

The decorative glass trade, especially that part which utilized coloured glasses, remained predominantly Alexandrian for a long period. Roman conquests in North Africa during the first century BC introduced a new luxury import to the capital: vessels carved from colourful hardstones. Of these the so-called murrhine cups were the most sought, and consequently the most expensive. The Alexandrians flooded the Roman market with imitations of hardstones in glass, made by pressing into moulds. Whether we can, from this scanty evidence, identify the hardstone vessels with those murrhine cups for which Caligula and Nero paid such vast sums is doubtful. One reference at least suggests that they came from the Middle East, from Parthia or beyond (Propertius. IV. 5. 26. *Murreaque in Parthis pocula cocta focis*).

The glass-houses of Italy appear to have been founded at a time when the technique of glass-blowing first appeared in that country, about 20 AD. The principal centres at Cumae and Liternum utilized the sand of the river Volturnus, which was especially suited to the purpose. A factory at Puteoli nearby was established about the same time, and glass-makers existed in Rome during the first century AD.

In Imperial times glass was employed extensively as decoration in the form of wall-tiles, especially in bathrooms, and as mosaics [figure 15]. In the days of Pliny the Elder the glass-mosaic was becoming increasingly popular as interior decoration, associated with mural painting and richly gilded ceilings. The finest and most detailed of these mosaics have been found at Hadrian's Villa at Tivoli.

Glass-workers were divided into *vitrearii*, who were blowers and moulders, and *diatretarii* responsible for cutting and engraving. The latter term, which seems to have been Alexandrian in origin, was later more or less confined to the makers of fantastically skilled openwork cutting to be found in the *diatreta*, or cage-cups, of which the finest surviving example is shown in figure 12. The greater number of these are in German museums. This limitation of the term, however, is unjustified, and it may correctly be employed to describe cutters and engravers of all kinds.

That the cage-cups were the work of migratory Alexan-

10 Square bottle blown into a mould, the handle added afterwards. Common domestic glass. Roman. First to third century AD

drian workmen is possible, although the decorative style shows no sign of eastern influence. An example of what is more likely to be Alexandrian work which is carved and undercut may be seen in figure 13.

Where the cage-cups were made is uncertain; it may have been in Rome itself or even in the Rhineland, although the work is much finer than anything else to be attributed to this region. The fantastic degree of patience, ingenuity, and skill exhibited is equalled only by such examples of fine cameo-cutting as the Portland vase. It has been suggested that the cage-cups were cut under water, which would greatly have reduced the risk of breakage and spalling. They began as vessels of cased glass, the patterns being pierced and undercut by the lapidary's wheel with an effect which may be studied in the illustration.

According to Fremersdorf's theory these cups were first made of solid glass thick enough to allow the decoration to be carved from it. They were then cut down in such a way as to leave two raised zones, the upper for the inscription, and the lower (hemispherical, and occupying about half the cup) for the cage-work. The lower zone was first bored with circular holes to the necessary depth, and the intervening glass then undercut to separate the upper layer from the vessel proper, leaving small supports between the two. The last operation was to abrade the remaining glass into the final shape. There is little doubt that this sequence of operations is the correct interpretation.

In the *diatreta* the art of the lapidary was carried to the ultimate limit of skill. Technically less spectacular but more important artistically are the finer surviving examples of cameo-cutting on glass vessels of one colour cased with another. The best known of this rare group is undoubtedly the Portland vase [figure 1], which began as a vase of a blue so dark that it is virtually black. This was flashed with an almost opaque white glass, and the lapidary cut the decoration through the white layer down to the blue. In parts he deliberately approached the blue layer so nearly that it has struck through the white, providing delicate shadowings to enhance the modelling. Elsewhere the white layer has been removed altogether.

The vase has a remarkable history. Once thought to have contained the ashes of the Emperor Alexander Severus (222–235 AD), it was in the possession of the Barberini family in Rome in 1642, and was then reputed to have been discovered enclosed in a marble sarcophagus about sixty years before. In 1780 it was bought by a Scottish art dealer living in Rome, who sold it to the English ambassador at Naples, Sir William Hamilton, a noted collector of classical antiquities and husband of Nelson's mistress. In turn Sir William sold it to the Duchess of Portland.

When the Duchess died in 1785 her collection was auctioned in London, and the vase was bought by her son, the Duke of Portland, for 980 guineas. Subsequently the Duke lent it to Josiah Wedgwood, who executed a number of copies in jasper-ware, and in 1810 it was lent to the British Museum. The Museum purchased it in 1945.

A reproduction commissioned by Philip Pargeter of Stourbridge and executed by John Northwood was made in glass in the 1870s, and this has provided us with some insight into the difficulties of the Roman cameo-cutters and glass-makers. Northwood took three years to complete his copy, which was undertaken only after he had gained some

11 Bowl in the form of a boat of moulded and carved glass, found at Pompeii. Before 79 A D

12 *Diatretglas* found in April 1960 in the Stolberger Strasse, Köln-Braunsfeld. The inscription reads: ΠΙΕ ΖΗΣΑΙΣ ΚΑΛΩΣ ΑΕΙ (Drink and live well also). Probably made for a Greek living in the Rhineland. Third to fourth century AD

years of experience in doing preliminary work of lesser importance. The first problem to be overcome was that presented by the differing contraction rates of the two layers. No fewer than seven attempts were needed to reproduce the vase itself.

An example of undercutting combined with cameo-cutting of detail which, in some ways, is even more complex than the cage-cups is illustrated in figure 13. It is evident that this work could not be separated into zones

17

followed by cutting operations which succeeded each other in logical sequence. The glass itself is an apparently olive-green in colour, but when held to the light it assumes a transparent purplish-red shade. This effect was probably accidental, and the result of an incomplete reduction of the copper oxide used to colour it, the original aim being to produce a red glass.

Roman engraving on clear and monochrome glass is variable in quality, ranging from fine work to less accomplished specimens intended for a cheaper market. These, done for the most part with the engraver's wheel, sometimes exhibit passages of diamond-engraving also. Occasionally diamond-engraving forms the only decoration. Much work of this kind is Alexandrian, and the enmity between engravers and glass-makers, as well marked in Rome as in eighteenth-century England, has been well-described by Guttery (*From Broad-glass to Cut Crystal*) referring to the situation at Stourbridge: 'These gaffers, master-work-men, had now perforce to pass on their "beautiful articles" to the grinders, unwelcome intruders, who, poisoning themselves with putty-powder and red lead and deafening their ears with the screams of their wheels, worked . . . on the same premises as the gaffer's eternal furnace fires'.

The 'gaffers' of Rome produced large quantities of transparent metal of excellent quality, blown, moulded, and cast, and they often decorated it with trailed threads in simple colours, or by tooling the softened glass. Their metal was never entirely colourless, but usually a pale green, with small air-bubbles and striations evident. Because of these defects much of it had colouring oxides added, especially those giving a deeper green or an amber.

A new departure in Rome was the introduction of enamels for painting on glass. These colours were made from a metallic oxide suspended in an organic medium and suitably fluxed. They needed a low-temperature firing to develop them. Enamelling in Rome was a late innovation apparently not often used, but an excellent example is in the Treasury of St Mark's in Venice, and another of the time of Constantine in the Römisch-Germanisches Museum at Cologne.

The 'gold sandwich' technique already mentioned was another late Roman adoption, and a fragmentary example is illustrated in figure 8. The origin is usually regarded as Alexandrian, but many specimens recovered have come from Roman catacombs and are decorated with Jewish and

13 Cup of olive-green glass carved and under-cut in a technique similar to that used for the cage-cups. The subject represents the madness of Lycurgus of Thrace. Perhaps Alexandrian. Late third century AD

Christian symbols. Whether or not this glass was also made in the Rhineland is debatable, but the technique was revived in a slightly different form in Germany during the early years of the eighteenth century [figure 71]. In favour of Alexandrian origin rather than Jewish is the fact that 'gold sandwich' glasses survived in Egypt until Islamic times, certain very rare Fatimid specimens (969–1164) being thus decorated.

What little information we have about Roman glass-manufacture up to the end of the first century AD comes from Pliny, who collected it together in his *Natural History*. A tantalizing reference to the production of 'flexible' glass during the reign of Tiberius probably refers to a kind of glass which was relatively unbreakable; it may have been made with a toughened exterior, like windscreen glass. Speculation, however, is useless because the workshop making it was destroyed to prevent the value of objects of copper, silver, and gold from depreciating. No specimens survive, and the story, according to Pliny, was more widely spread than well-authenticated.

'Obsian' glass, described by Pliny, was an imitation of the natural volcanic glass, obsidian. He refers to a statue of Augustus in solid material, but whether he means obsidian proper or the glass imitation is not entirely clear. This, however, is the source of later reports of glass statues in Imperial times.

According to Seneca 'a man esteemed himself very poor who had not his room surrounded with sheets of glass', and the largest sheet of window-glass of which we have knowledge measured forty inches by twenty-eight inches, and was half an inch thick. Pliny refers to mirrors as being an invention of the Sidonian glass-houses, although the glass may have been dark in colour, resembling obsidian, reflecting – as Pliny comments – 'the shadow rather than the image'. In an obscure and possibly corrupt passage in Book XXXIII. Chap. 45, he appears to say that experiments had been made by backing mirrors either with gold foil or with an amalgam of gold and mercury, the latter being in common use for gilding copper.

A blood-red glass referred to as *haematinum* was employed for table-services, as well as white glass, sapphire glass, and 'every other tint'. But the greatest value was set upon glass which was entirely transparent, as nearly as possible like crystal. Of this kind perhaps were two small cups made by a new process called 'petroti', for which the

14 Urn-shaped vase of light green metal, the foot drawn out from the base. Perhaps Alexandrian. Third to fourth century AD

19

Emperor Nero paid six thousand sesterces (perhaps £350 in today's currency). A better reading might be *pterotos*, with winged handles, which suggests something like the much later Venetian goblets [figure 30]. *Haematinum* appears to be the first attested glass containing lead oxide as a flux, although lead had already been included in pottery glazes. An analysis by Pettenkofer, who succeeded in reproducing *haematinum*, revealed fifteen per cent of lead, with the addition of cuprous oxide as the colouring agent.

Most ancient glass develops a rainbow-like iridescence, similar to the appearance of petrol spilled on a wet road, as a result of prolonged burial. An unusually fine example of this effect is shown in figure 16. Iridescence is caused by the interaction of the surface with carbonic acid, and it is a decomposition which, in extreme cases, may penetrate much more deeply, rendering a thin glass exceedingly fragile. Great age and long burial are usually necessary for the development of the kind of iridescence shown, but new glass is sometimes given a fairly deceptive appearance of this kind by immersing it in a cesspool for a few months.

The use of unrefined materials causes transparent glass to which no colouring oxides have been added to assume a well-marked but pale tinge of green, bluish-green, smoky-grey, or yellow. Alexandrian glass often exhibits a slight purplish tinge when manganese has been used as a de-colourizer. Reproductions usually show a stronger shade of these colour tinges more evenly distributed, since the colour (nearly always green) has been added and does not arise

15 A rare small mosaic of Pompeian type made from glass *tesserae* embedded in cement (*opus sectile*). First century AD

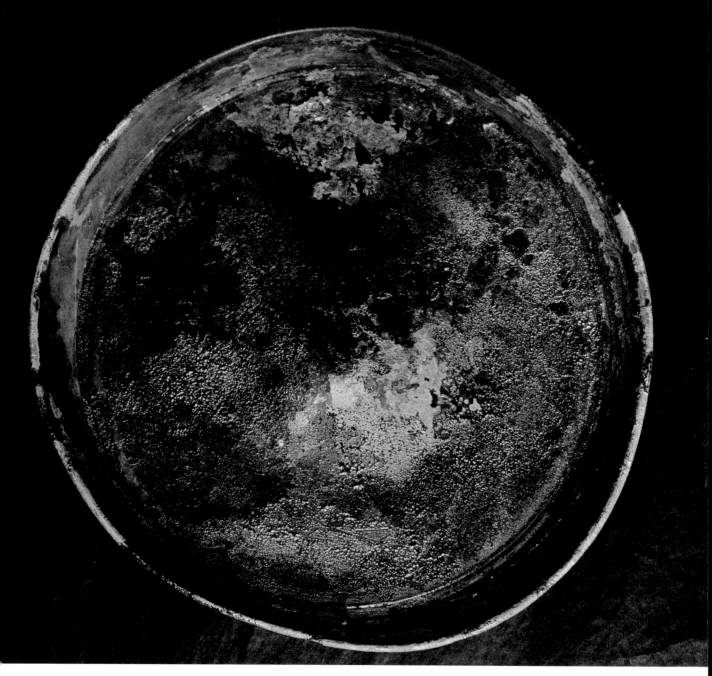

16 Small Roman dish with unusually fine iridescence. First to third century AD

from natural causes.

It will be apparent from what has already been written that all the principal ways of manufacturing and decorating glass were known to ancient glass-makers, and only one minor technique, that of glass-etching, had to wait for the discovery of hydrofluoric acid by the Swedish chemist, Scheele, towards the end of the eighteenth century.

When the focus of the industry began to shift from

17 Ampulla of light amber-coloured metal blown into a mould. The mould-seam is clearly visible. Probably Syrian. First to third century AD

Rome to Byzantium in the fourth century there were no technical innovations of importance. Changes were those of style, and at first this is only evident when Christian symbols appear in the decoration. The use of glass in ecclesiastical ritual belongs to the early centuries of Christianity, a fifth century example – a chalice in blue glass from Amiens – which is characteristic of a very rare group being illustrated here [figure 36]. The Byzantine 'gold sandwich' glasses were probably made entirely for domestic use, since they occur with both Christian and pagan *motifs*.

Moulded glass vessels are known with Christian symbols in relief, and the fish blown into a mould has this connotation. Cameos began to be produced in moulds, a commercial development of the earlier work of Roman lapidaries, and Byzantine enamelling provides a bridge between Roman and later Islamic work of this kind.

There is hardly space to examine mosaic, which is probably the most important aspect of Byzantine art. Mosaics were largely composed of small pieces of variously coloured glass *(tesserae)* embedded in a cement matrix. The use of a backing of gold foil to enhance the splendour of the designs is allied in technique to the 'gold sandwich' glass. The immense labour and cost of such works may be deduced from the calculation that the mosaics of the dome of the Church of St George at Salonika needed thirty-six million separately affixed *tesserae* to complete them.

How widely the actual manufacture of glass was distributed throughout the Roman Empire is a question difficult to answer. Forms are often remarkably similar, and of the specimens recovered many were undoubtedly imported. Manufacture was well established at several centres in Gaul by the end of the first century BC, and at Cologne in the Rhineland where especially suitable beds of sand were not far away. The most frequent recoveries of importance are cinerary urns, which were given the protection of stone containers.

The glass-works of Cologne in particular were flourishing as late as the fourth century AD, when they were granted special tax-reliefs by Constantine. Apart from the remarkable cage-cups already discussed, which may have been made at Cologne, the greater part of production was devoted to vessels of domestic utility. These were made in large quantities throughout the province of Gaul, and they were often stamped with the name of the owner of the glass-house. The earlier use of cattle-horns as drinking-vessels is responsible for some glass vessels made in the same form [figure 31].

Soda-glass of greenish transparency, or coloured with metallic oxides, was made in Spain from the early years of the present era, and by the third century simple wheel-engraved patterns decorated both funerary and domestic wares. The source of soda, burning plants derived from the salt-marshes, provided also a source of lime in small quantities. Elsewhere glass-makers had discovered the part played by lime, which made the metal stronger, more durable, and less likely to deteriorate in contact with water, and they were adding it in larger quantities.

The glass industry in Britain was on a very small scale during Roman times, and most specimens recovered were probably imported. Window-glass has been found at Silchester, and it is possible that simple engraving was done in Britain, perhaps on imported glass. A very rare vessel of the late Roman period has a decoration of hollow lobes pointing downwards, in form a little like an elephant's head and trunk, placed at intervals round the exterior. This is the apparent origin of the so-called 'claw-beaker' of Anglo-Saxon times in England, represented here by a specimen found at Castle Eden in Co Durham [figures 7 and 19]. At Faversham in Kent, and at other places in the south of England, conical beakers in blue, green, and amber glass, sometimes fluted and sometimes with a decoration of trailed threads, as well as globular vessels with a short expanding neck, have been recovered. Few were provided with the means to stand upright, and the contents were intended to be emptied at a draught. A conical variety was obviously based on the drinking-horn. These vessels are of coarser metal than the better quality Roman wares, commonly showing numerous bubbles and striations. They are also more prone to have deteriorated as the result of burial.

The general form of these drinking-cups is not a good guide to the place of origin. Other finds of Frankish or Teutonic glass in Germany vary only a little from that found in England, and the relationship is clear enough, as well as the line of descent. There is, in fact, little evidence of glass-making in England of any kind during the medieval period, and on the Continent the craft survived only in a debased form, although knowledge of it was preserved from earlier times in written form by the alchemists who copied from Pliny and others.

18 Small bowl of clear glass. Frankish or Teutonic. About sixth century AD

23

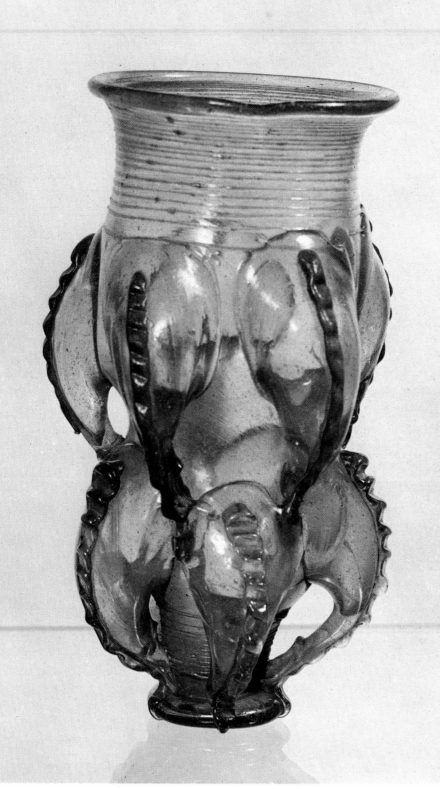

⊕riental glass

19 *(left)* Claw-beaker found at Castle Eden, Co Durham, and representative of a type found also in the South of England at Faversham, and in Germany. Frankish glass. Probably seventh century AD

20 Horse carved in glass using a hardstone technique. China. T'ang dynasty (618–906 AD)

IT WAS FOR LONG thought that glass was not made in China until the fifth century AD. The authority for this view was derived from Chinese literary sources which discuss imports of coloured glass from the west in the third century. The extent of the trade may be judged from the occurrence of Roman and Near Eastern glass in the ninth century art collection housed in the Shoso-in Pavilion at Nara, the old capital of Japan, and blown glass vessels have been recovered from Japanese tombs of the fifth century.

So late a date, however, must now be regarded as erroneous, and glass was undoubtedly known in China towards the end of the Chou dynasty (1122–249 BC), when it occurs in the form of a glass-paste inlay on certain bronze vessels. There is little or no chance of any of these early occurrences being imported glass subsequently powdered and remelted, since Chinese glass contains barium and this does not appear in any known variety of Western glass.

The Chinese regarded glass as a kind of rock-crystal transmuted from sand by the agency of fire, and the earliest products copied ritual jades, especially such carvings as the cicada and the *pi*, the circular symbol of Heaven. The proportion of blown glass which appears even in the eighteenth century is very small, and most glass was employed as a kind of hardstone, like jade, agate, and rock-crystal, and decorated by carving with abrasives [figure 20].

There is little reliable information relating to glass made before the beginning of the Ch'ing dynasty (1644–1912), but a small quantity of blown glass is probably referable to the reign of the Emperor K'ang Hsi (1662–1722). It is not, perhaps, too fanciful to see in some of it a resemblance to certain kinds of Venetian glass.

Early Ch'ing blown glass suffers from the same defect as certain European glass of the period, a progressive deterioration termed 'crisselling' [figures 21 and 105]. This term refers to the development of a network of fine cracks, often associated with the appearance of an unpleasantly smelling liquid on the surface, which leads eventually to varying degrees of decomposition. The cause is obscure. It probably begins with the condensation of water on the glass, which dissolves some of the silicates. When it dries the surface is left with a multitude of tiny

25

21 Bowl of crisselled glass. China. Reign of the Emperor K'ang Hsi (1662–1722)

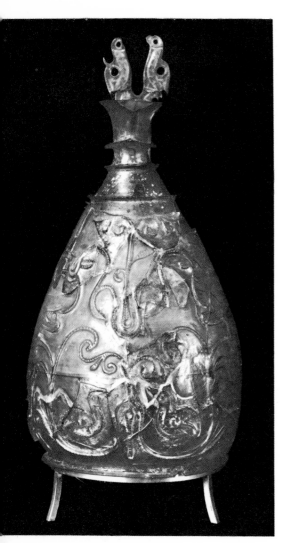

22 Ewer, reconstructed from fragments, carved in deep relief perhaps from a block of glass in the technique used for making rock-crystal vessels. Probably Egyptian. End of tenth century AD

cracks, and eventually minute flakes of glass begin to fall from it. The remedy seems to be to keep the affected specimen in carefully regulated atmospheric conditions. Crisselling is related in its effect to the formation of iridescence, although the cause is different.

Most glass of the Ch'ing dynasty was cast into moulds, and for this reason it is heavier than comparable European work. It is nearly always coloured, and, remembering their remarkable skill in the use of metallic oxides for decorating porcelain, it is hardly surprising that the Chinese produced glass in a large range of excellent colours. Cased glass was commonly made, sometimes three layers through which lapidaries carved designs reminiscent of lacquer-work.

Few carved objects are large, and most frequent are miniature snuff-bottles, an inch or two in height, on which much skill was lavished. Glass snuff-bottles of this kind strongly recall the art of the jade-carver, and delicate *intaglio* engraving is present on some of them. Some rare specimens of glass have painted scenes on the *inside*, the brush being introduced through the narrow neck. Large glass sheets, as well as mirrors, were also employed as a support for paintings in oil or gouache colours – a technique developed principally for export, the decoration often with western designs, or with a fusion of these and oriental *motifs*.

Perhaps the most sought examples of Chinese decoration on glass are the opaque white vases in forms imitating porcelain, delicately painted with soft enamels like their porcelain counterparts, either with European subjects or

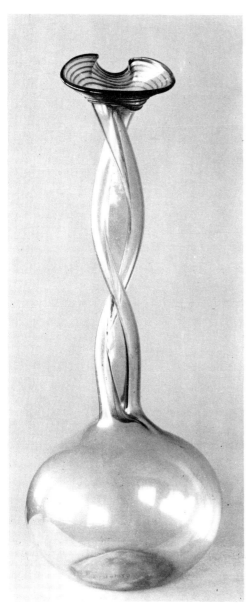

23 Venetian sprinkler-bottle of the seventeenth century for comparison with the Persian bottle figure 24

with those calculated to appeal to the European market. An example appears in figure 37. This rare group is termed Ku-yuëh Hsüan (Ancient Moon Pavilion) because this is the translation of the characters found on some of them. Specimens belong either to the reign of Yung Chêng (1723–35) or to the very early years of Ch'ien Lung who followed him. It is possible that painting of this kind on glass preceded its appearance on porcelain. For the most part glass in China must be regarded as a branch of jade and hardstone carving rather than as an independent art.

It is probable that the introduction of the secret of glass-making into China came from Near Eastern sources. The road between China and the Near East was certainly open in the time of Alexander the Great, when Chinese silk was first exported westwards, and the history of these early interchanges between eastern and western Asia has still to be written.

The rise of Islam in the seventh century AD, and the rapid conquest of Palestine, Persia, and North Africa which followed, was accompanied by the spread of new ideas in glass-making, no doubt developments of the work of the old Syrian glass-makers, since Syria was among the earliest of the territories to fall under the sway of the new religion. Damascus, Tyre, and Antioch all retained a reputation for glass-working, including wheel-engraving, for which we have the authority of the Jewish traveller, Benjamin of Tudela. Glass vessels 'in the fashion of Damascus' appear in the Royal Inventories of France in the fourteenth century, although the description may refer to Islamic glass generally rather than to that of Damascus.

The glass-making tradition of Alexandria survived in Egypt in a diminished form, and glass weights have been recovered in large numbers from the rubbish-heaps of Old Cairo (Fostat). There are early references from Islamic sources to the excellence of Egyptian glass. These Saracens, to give the adherents of Islam the name by which they were commonly known in Europe during the Middle Ages, were probably in touch with Byzantine craftsmen, some of whom may have emigrated to territories under Islamic domination. Here many of the older Alexandrian techniques had been preserved, and Byzantium was probably the origin of both gilding and enamelling later used with such superb effect by Saracen workmen. The art of glass-blowing remained common property.

Although the Saracens learned the art of enamelling in

27

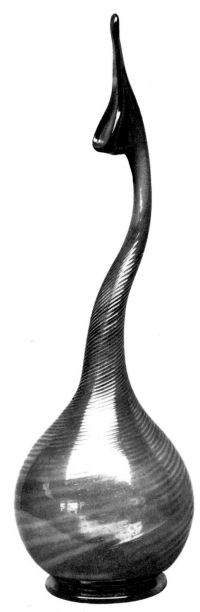

24 Persian sprinkler-bottle. *Façon de Venise.*
End of the seventeenth century

several colours and could produce enamel grounds of excellent quality, the metal was usually deficient, the transparency exhibiting tinges of colour associated with unrefined and impure materials, with both bubbles and striations. In fact, the art of making a good metal clear of such imperfections was never mastered, except perhaps at Old Cairo, where fragments of a better quality are sometimes found.

Coloured glass windows were often used in mosques and the better private houses of Egypt — red, blues, greens, and yellows — but, unlike European work, the metal was coloured throughout with the usual oxides rather than stained or enamelled. Glass mosaics were used for such places as the prayer-niches of mosques. But the true glory of Islamic glass resides in the enamelled mosque lamps (actually lamp-containers) which begin in the middle of the fourteenth century, and the even rarer vessels similarly decorated, some of which are referable to the thirteenth century. Much of this kind of work came from Syria, and the style of decoration is closely allied to inlaid bronzework from Mosul, and to a lesser extent to the enamelled pottery of Persia known as *minai*.

The origin of this kind of enamelling is obscure. The goblet illustrated in figure 78, probably brought back to Europe by Crusading marauders before 1291, is related to several others still existing. The actual enamelling has been claimed for Venice, but it may have been executed by a Venetian workman employed by a Syrian glass-enamelling establishment. The existence of Christian workmen at Islamic manufactories is well established. The well-known 'Luck of Edenhall' [figure 79], if its fourteenth century leather case be accepted as a reliable guide, has been in England since the end of that century.

The mosque lamp especially was frequently decorated with Saracenic coats of arms, which enable many of them to be dated fairly accurately. The European fashion for such arms was probably derived from Saracen sources, brought back by Crusaders, and those of the Mamluk Sultans appear fairly frequently. Inscriptions are also common, usually arranged in bands in the angular and formal Kufic script. Most such inscriptions refer to the Sultan in adulatory terms — for instance, 'Glory to our lord the Sultan, the King, the Illustrious, whom God assist' — and pious verses from the Koran are also to be noticed. One example, almost certainly of Damascus make, refers directly to the lamp and the manner of its use: 'God is the light of the heavens and the earth; his light is as a niche in which is a lamp, and the lamp in a glass; the glass as it were a glittering star.' The enamelled lamps were made to be suspended from a ceiling rather than placed in a niche, but the reference quoted otherwise testifies to their importance.

Work of this kind was already in decline towards the end of the fourteenth century when the Mongol conqueror, Tamerlane, looted Damascus and removed many of its workmen to his own city of Samarkand. The rise of Venice as the great trading port of the eastern Mediterranean, and the development of its glass industry, probably prevented any revival.

25 A *jeu d'esprit* of a Persian 'gaffer' – a glass mouse made 'at the lamp'. Eighteenth century

Little is known of the manufacture of glass in Persia and Mesopotamia before the seventeenth century, and in general the attribution of Near Eastern glass of the early period to a *place* of origin is always hazardous. Excavations at Samarra on the Tigris, the site of the summer palace of the Caliph Mu'tasim erected in 838 and destroyed in 883, have brought to light numerous fragments of glass, but, unlike the pottery sherds recovered in the same place, these do not tell us very much about their origin. Probably some are Syrian and others of Egyptian manufacture, or made by immigrant workmen in the style of those regions. The argument which would attribute the cut and engraved fragments found at Samarra to a Persian centre of manufacture by analogy with Sassanian carved rock-crystal is not sufficiently strong to be convincing, and, although contemporary sources refer to the glass of Iraq, Egypt or Syria are perhaps the more likely.

The lustre painting of Persian and Egyptian pottery, that is painting in pigments derived from very finely powdered silver, gold, and copper, is also to be found on glass of the eleventh century, especially on fragments excavated in Egypt [figure 26].

The manufacture of glass in Persia began once more on a noteworthy scale during the reign of Shah Abbas (1587 to 1628), when Venetian glass was also imported. It is known that Venetian workmen were present at Shiraz, the principal glassmaking centre, and bottles with slender curved necks and an expanded mouth, in blue, purple, brownish-yellow, and a bluish copper green, are not uncommon. Figures 23 and 24 compare a Persian bottle of this kind with one of a slightly earlier date made in Venice.

26 Glass bowl painted with lustre pigment of the kind found on contemporary pottery. Egypt. Eleventh century

29

Venice

28 Top of a glass bowl on a low foot, enamelled with the Medici Arms surmounted by the Papal tiara and keys (either Leo X or Clement XVIII). *c.* 1520

27 *(left)* A Venetian glass ewer in the form of a *nef* (a ship used as a table centre-piece). The rigging is of blue and gilt trellis work. Lion-masks in relief. *c.* 1520

THE ORIGIN OF THE great Italian centre of glass-making at Venice cannot be traced with certainty much farther back than the tenth century. There remains, however, the possibility that the industry was carried on before this date on a small scale, especially for the manufacture of *tesserae* for glass mosaics inspired by those of Ravenna. Glass for this purpose was undoubtedly imported also from Byzantine sources. In 1291 the Senate decreed that, because of the increasing risk of fire from the number of furnaces operating, the industry be removed from the Rialto to the Island of Murano. The evolution of the industry may be studied in the Museo dell'Arte Vetraria in the Palazzo Comunale, and the Murano glass-blower largely retains the skill of his republican forebears.

The position of Venice until the Renaissance was unique. Its site has always been virtually impregnable from the sea or by land, at least until the development of modern weapons, and its merchants for most of the time ignored the edicts of the Pope and traded freely with the Saracens, not only in the natural and manufactured products of Islam, but in those of China, brought along the old Silk Road by caravan and redistributed overland to Antwerp and beyond. It was no accident that the first Europeans to reach the Court of Kublai Khan, the Yüan emperor of China, were the Venetian family of Polo, of whom the nephew, Marco, has left us an account of his travels. The influence of the east is rarely far away in any Venetian product, especially those made earlier than the sixteenth century, and as late as the early years of the eighteenth century Venetian harbour-scenes, with exotically turbaned figures, decorated Meissen porcelain.

Venetian glass-makers were in touch with Alexandria (where the old traditions still lingered) during the twelfth century, and the influence of Syria is also very strong, especially in the soda-glass produced from the excellent beds of pebbly sand nearby, to which was added the ashes of marine plants, at first obtained locally and then imported from Spain. Some remarks on the effect of using soda-glass on forms and techniques of decoration have already been made; its plastic qualities led especially to the extensive

29 *Tazza* of greyish metal, the scale decoration in gold outlined with spots of coloured enamels, the rim and foot strengthened by folding over while soft. Venice. Sixteenth century

30 Two-handled vase, the form showing traces of Near Eastern influence. Venice. Sixteenth century

use of trailed ornament, and of glass worked in a softened state with such tools as pincers, which characterizes much Venetian glass from the sixteenth century onwards. It is often difficult to date closely in the absence of a specific technique or mode of decoration which may, for one reason or another, be assigned to a particular period.

The concentration of the industry on the Island of Murano led to monopoly under the aegis of the Republic, and glass-workers gained eventually in prestige. The assertion that, by virtue of their craft, they achieved a social position which made them generally acceptable in marriage to Venetian noble families is a legend with little foundation in fact, although a nobleman was able to marry the daughter of a glass-worker with the legal assurance that his title could be transmitted to his progeny, and gentlemen could also engage in the trade without loss of status or distinction.

The monopolists were anxious to preserve their manufacturing secrets, and severe penalties were enjoined for absconding workmen. According to Labarte, the Statutes of the State Inquisition about the middle of the sixteenth century contained the following provisions: If a workman absconded an order was first to be sent to him to return. If he did not obey his nearest relatives were to be committed to prison. If, in spite of this, he persisted in remaining abroad, an assassin was to be sent to kill him. Two such cases are recorded in the Venetian archives, but no doubt there were more. These draconian restrictions were still in existence in the middle of the eighteenth century, when they were confirmed.

Despite this, some glass-makers escaped to join a rival centre at Altare, near Savona and not far from Genoa. Others went to France, England, Spain, Germany, and the Netherlands, and it is often difficult to decide where a particular specimen was made, so closely do they resemble each other in style and metal. Venice itself received assistance from immigrant workmen. The fall of Byzantium in 1204, when it was stormed and looted by marauding Crusaders, brought fugitive glass-makers to Venice, and in 1453, the year in which Byzantium was captured by the Turkish armies, more workmen made their way there.

Towards the end of the fifteenth century it first becomes possible to attribute specimens with a fair measure of certainty, especially some extremely rare pedestal-footed goblets decorated with enamels, a technique inspired by Syrian

31 Drinking-horn of amber glass. Frankish.
Sixth to seventh century AD

sources [figure 29]. Some of the earliest specimens are Gothic in style, others are obviously inspired by Near Eastern metalwork. Yet other forms were suggested by contemporary Italian silver.

Enamelled goblets, which were often gilded also, remained fashionable until the end of the first quarter of the sixteenth century. The earliest were painted with portraits (much more rarely with processions) on blue glass, the border patterns being executed in raised enamel dots, like gems. A dotted fish-scale border is reminiscent of a similar *motif* found on the *maiolica* of Faenza made about 1480 [figure 29]. After 1500 enamelled glass tends to be more simply decorated, principally with shields of arms and *motifs* of the period [figure 28]. Some confusion between these and similar glasses enamelled in Germany has occurred, and these are discussed later.

Decorating glass by engraving with a diamond began

33

32 Pilgrim-bottle, *vitro di trina* technique
Venice. Late sixteenth century

about 1560, and the fashion was soon freely adopted elsewhere. Within twenty years, for instance, it had travelled as far afield as London, where it was employed to decorate glasses made by Jacopo Verzelini (or James Verselyne), a Venetian appearing in an Elizabethan patent of 1575, who produced 'drynkynge glasses such as be accustomablie made in the towne of Morano'. Venetian glass decorated with diamond-engraving is extremely rare, and most specimens of this nature come from elsewhere [figure 38].

Enamelling was abandoned, and diamond-engraving adopted, because of the development of a better quality glass. Early Venetian metal suffered from the common defects of most soda-glass, especially bubbles and striations. There was also a marked tendency towards discolouration, and it was not until the fifteenth century that the old process of adding manganese to overcome this fault was rediscovered. The improved metal of the sixteenth century was called 'cristallo'; this was an allusion to its resemblance to the much-valued rock-crystal, a hardstone which frequently influenced styles adopted by Renaissance glass-workers, and the term 'crystal' for clear metal of good quality has been common since.

The development of an opaque but translucent white glass was inevitable. This, made by adding tin oxide to the crucible, was already well known, since it is indistinguishable from the normal *maiolica* glaze. White glass of this kind superficially resembled Chinese porcelain, then being imported into Europe in small quantities and highly valued. Instances of white glass being used elsewhere as a porcelain substitute are not uncommon, and, as a line of research, white glass culminated in the artificial porcelain of Florence about 1580 – the so-called Medici porcelain – in which ground glass was allied to clay to produce a substance which could be shaped by means appropriate to the potter. There is record of a Venetian attempt at porcelain-making along the same lines, but nothing now survives in a recognizable form, and the Venetians seem to have made little use of white glass for this purpose at the time. A later specimen of glass enamelled in the manner of porcelain is illustrated in figure 90.

The use of trailed threads of glass developed into a mode of decoration in which canes were used to form complex interlacing patterns, the finer of which were called *vitro di trina* from the resemblance to lacework, *latticino* or *latticinio* being more general terms. These canes, set in a

33 A glass lamp decorated in the *latticino* technique. Venice. Sixteenth century

34 and 35 (*left*) Bouquetier in blue and clear glass. (*right*) Vase with a body in the form of a scallop shell and blue glass handles. Venice. Seventeenth century

matrix of clear glass, were the forerunners of the white and coloured 'twists' to be found decorating the stems of eighteenth-century wine-glasses [figures 32 and 33]. Glass of this kind became extremely popular, reaching England by 1542.

Once the broad principle had been established, many variations were devised on the original theme, from the simplest to the building up of vessels using white and coloured canes, sometimes one layer over the other, twisting in opposite directions. The only limits were set by the ingenuity of the craftsmen in manipulating and drawing out the softened material.

Side by side with this use of softened canes may be found such *tours de force* of the glass-maker's art as the elaborately convoluted stems of goblets manipulated and formed with pincers [figure 34]. These kinds of decorative glass are, perhaps, the ultimate in skill to which the glass-maker, as distinct from the painter and the engraver, could

35

36 Blue glass vase, probably intended for a chalice, found near Amiens. About fifth century AD

37 (opposite) Small vase of an elegant porcelain form painted in the Ku-yuëh Hsüan style. China. Mid-eighteenth century

aspire, and it is these for which Venice is famed. The manufacture of *latticino* glass persisted well into the eighteenth century, and elaborately trailed work into the nineteenth. Both varieties in fact are still sometimes made at Murano.

Not only the simulation of rock-crystal but the reproduction of coloured hardstones had been an important goal of the glass-maker since the florescence of Alexandrian manufacture. An eighteenth-century writer on the subject says: 'The *Chemists* hold that there is no Body but may be *vitrified*, that is, converted into *Glass* . . . and it was a merry Saying of a very great Artist in the Business of

38 Dish with the Arms of Pius IV in gold in the centre, the remainder decorated with diamond-point engraving. Between the bands of engraving, on the underside, are gilt lines edged with white glass. *c.* 1560

39 Stoppered vessel and bowl of ice-glass. Venice. Sixteenth century

Glass that their Profession would be the last in the World; for that when God should consume the Universe with Fire, all things there in would be turned to Glass.' Certainly most hardstones were regarded as a kind of glass, in which the only essential difference was a greater degree of hardness. It is not surprising, therefore, to find glasses resembling jasper, onyx, agate, and chalcedony (the type is sometimes referred to as *calcedonio*) being produced at an early date, perhaps at the beginning of the fifteenth century [figure 40]. Most such glass (often termed *Schmelz* glass) belongs to the sixteenth century and later, and it continued to be made until the eighteenth. The suspension in glass of tiny flakes of metallic copper, imitating the plates of mica in aventurine quartz which give it the characteristic gold-spangled appearance, was then a speciality of the Miotti family. This rare type of glass was also made in China during the eighteenth century.

Ice-glass is an unusual technique employed during the sixteenth century. Buckley (*The Art of Glass*) says that a bubble of glass was plunged while still hot into water, and then immediately reheated and blown. This had the effect of imparting to the surface innumerable small cracks and fissures, which gave an appearance of frosting. Rolling the

40 Goblet of *Schmelz* or *calcedonio* glass imitating jasper. Venice. Early sixteenth century

vessel while still soft in splintered glass yielded a similar effect. Specimens are rare, and much the same type was made at Liège also, making attribution to one place or another difficult [figure 39].

The so-called *millefiore* (thousand-flower) glass was a revival in Venice of the old Roman and Alexandrian method of building up vessels from cross-sections of coloured canes [figure 5], and another ancient technique — blowing into moulds — was employed during the sixteenth and seventeenth centuries for vases.

Especially during the seventeenth century mirrors formed a large part of Venetian production, and they had been made since the early years of the sixteenth century at least. Even as late as 1770 a sheet of mirror-glass measuring five feet by three feet six inches cost £80 in England — equivalent to about £800 in today's money. The great Galérie des Glaces of Versailles, with its seventeen arches filled with 360 Venetian mirrors in bronze frames by Cucci, cost so much that Colbert founded the Manufacture Royale des Glaces de Miroirs to make mirror-glass in France, but the project was abandoned because of the difficulty experienced in finding Venetian workmen to provide the essential knowledge.

The opening of sea-routes to the Far East by way of the Cape greatly reduced the importance of Venice as a centre of Oriental trade on which its prosperity had been largely based, and the seventeenth century became a period of decline in glass-making, as in most other Venetian industries.

The eighteenth century saw the adoption of novelty for its own sake, and of attempts to follow fashion instead of to lead it. Enamelled white glass in imitation of porcelain was produced in the workshop of Daniele Miotti, and the Museo dell'Arte Vetraria has a small snuff-bottle initialled by him and dated 1767. A more ambitiously painted plate from the same workshop is in the Victoria and Albert Museum. A lively and primitive style characterizes enamelling from the workshop of the Brussa family.

Openwork baskets built up from trailed glass often have touches of colour. These were made also at Liège, and are sometimes erroneously attributed to Bristol. Baskets of coloured fruits, glass fruits on a tiered stand, and fruit inside a bottle blown around it, are all typical of the late eighteenth-century striving for novelty. Distinctly unusual is the occurrence of glass in various colours as inlay to an

41 Cup of white glass painted in the manner of porcelain in the Ku-yuëh Hsüan style. China. Mid-eighteenth century

ebonized cabinet (much in the same way as the porcelain of Sèvres was used in Paris and the jasper plaques of Wedgwood in England), but an example is preserved in the Museo Vetrario.

Small pieces, perhaps to be classified as a kind of *jeu d'esprit* in which glass-makers everywhere sometimes indulged, take the form of human figures, small animals, and sometimes more eccentric shapes. They date from the seventeenth century onwards, and were made 'at the lamp' – that is, by softening glass in a flame and manipulating it with pincers and similar tools. They are rare, because until glass-collecting became fashionable little serious effort was made to preserve them.

Much of the glass in the style of Venice (the *façon de Venise*) made elsewhere in Europe during the sixteenth and seventeenth centuries especially, often owed its existence, at least in the first place, to Venetian workmen. To give a full list of all such places in the present work would be tedious, but the characteristic style of Venice is to be seen in glass made in France, Germany, the Netherlands, Spain, and England. The most important centres are to be sought in Antwerp, Liège, Hall (near Innsbruck), Munich, Nürnberg, and London.

42 Chinese glass. Bowl of yellow glass with carved decoration. Mark and reign of the Emperor Ch'ien Lung (1736–96)

43 *(above) Façon de Venise. Latticino* vase and cover perhaps from Cassel. Late sixteenth century

44 *(above right)* Vase of clear glass, the opaque white figure in the interior astride a bulb of blue glass. Venice. Late seventeenth century

In France, glass in the Frankish tradition continued to be made in what was to become Normandy until the ninth century, when, perhaps as a result of the disturbances which followed the death of Charlemagne and the raids of the Northmen, the workers migrated to Altare, where they came under Syrian influence. From the middle of the fifteenth century onwards they spread out slowly through Europe taking their art with them, since, unlike the Venetians, they were not concerned to preserve it as a secret process. At this time production at Altare was virtually indistinguishable from that of Venice, and the difficulty frequently extends to those centres receiving their knowledge from either place.

The Altarists began their return to France towards the end of the thirteenth century, while the glass-workers of the Rhineland (the earlier Lotharingia) had persisted in Lorraine, making a simple domestic ware, greenish in colour, known as *verre de fougère* (forge-glass), analogous to the German *Waldglas*. In France the making of orna-

45 *Biberon*, an invalid feeding-bottle in which the spout is the only opening. Venice. Seventeenth century

46 *Façon de Venise*. A flute having a knop moulded with the Venetian lion-mask. Netherlandish. Sixteenth century

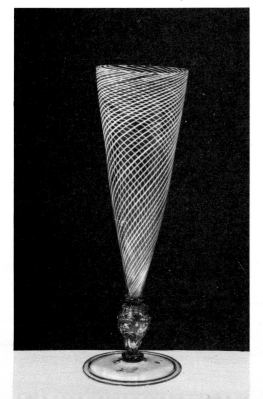

mental glass was rare until much later, although the art of stained glass was developed to a high degree of quality to fill the large window-openings possible with the developing Gothic style in architecture.

The principal divergence between the techniques of the glass-workers of Lorraine and those of Normandy is to be found in their sheet-glass. That of Lorraine was blown into a bubble which was rolled into a cylinder on the marver. While still soft the ends of the cylinder were cut off, after which it was slit down the centre and opened out. In Normandy, on the other hand, glass was gathered on the end of the pipe and rotated rapidly to make a disc with a thickened central boss. Glass made by the latter method is usually comparatively small in diameter, but a specimen in the Henry Francis Dupont Museum at Winterthur, Delaware, has a diameter of more than forty inches.

The glass-houses of Antwerp, set up before the middle of the sixteenth century, were principally influenced by Venice, since records speak of workers from Murano; however, those of Liège (started about thirty years later) owed their origin to the Altarists, although styles are closely similar. At Hall, in the Tirol, a beginning had been made even earlier, in 1534, and the glass-houses of Munich and Nürnberg followed in the course of the next few decades. The industry existed at Cassel, in the Province of Hesse, in 1584 [figure 43]. In England there is record of Venetian glass being imported in 1398 but nothing survives, and Henry VIII had a collection of Venetian goblets, some of which were mounted in gold and silver, as the Syrian glass brought back by the Crusaders had already been mounted, and as Chinese porcelain and Isnik faience were treated during the Tudor period.

Eight glass-blowers from Murano arrived in London in 1549 and established a workshop at Crutched Friars, near the Tower of London, where Verzelini, who had come to London by way of Antwerp, worked from 1575 onwards. Since Verzelini was given a monopoly of glass-making in 1575, the very rare specimens in the Venetian style which bear dates after this may be safely regarded as the work of London makers, although the metal closely resembles that used in Venice during the same period.

The export of Venetian glass to the eastern Mediterranean countries was on a fairly large scale, and some remarks on its influence on seventeenth century Persian manufacture have already been made.

Germany and the Netherlands

48 An unusual example of *chinoiserie* and *Laub-und Bandelwerk*, subjects much more familiar on Meissen porcelain. Wheel-engraved by Anton Wilhelm Maurel of Nürnberg (1672–1737)

47 *(left)* Enamelled mosque lamp bearing the name of Kijlis, Arms-Bearer to the Sultan am-Nasir Muhammad. The inscription reads: 'This is dedicated by a servant of God the Exalted, hoping for the pardon of his generous Lord Kijlis, Officer of al-Malik am-Nasir'. Probably Syrian. *c.* 1313

THE MAKING OF GLASS in Germany survived the troubled centuries which followed the collapse of the Roman Empire. Known as *Waldglas* (forest glass), it was made in small glass-houses conveniently situated near the source of wood-fuel. The metal was inferior in quality, although manipulation was skilful. The industry began to show signs of revival on a larger scale in the fifteenth century, and a characteristic survival from this period is the *Igel* (hedgehog beaker) decorated with spots of glass drawn out to a point, reminiscent of the old 'claw beakers'. Drinking-vessels of *Waldglas* appear in the old German records as *Krautstrunk* ('cabbage-stalk' glasses), *Warzenbecher* (wart or nipple beakers), and *Nuppenbecher*, the latter a term of uncertain meaning [figure 51].

By the beginning of the sixteenth century signs of Italian influence may easily be perceived, and this is to be expected because Germany, Austria and Bohemia (now Czechoslovakia) all formed part of the Holy Roman Empire. German glass-makers, however, speedily infused a distinctively national style into their work. Some seventeenth-century vessels were much influenced by the *Pokal*, a favourite of such South German silversmiths as Wenzel Jamnitzer. The *Pokal* is a large covered goblet, the latter term meaning a drinking-vessel holding more than four ounces of liquid [figure 65].

From the middle of the sixteenth century onwards the most popular kind of glass decoration was enamelling; the technique derived from Murano but the painting is in a distinctively German style. The earliest dated example – these fortunately are not unusual – was made in 1541, and they fall into several well-marked categories. The *Stangengläser* ('pole' glasses, so called from their tall cylindrical form) evolved into the *Humpen* (tankard). The *Walzenhumpen* (cylindrical tankard) was commonly painted with the arms and attributes of the lesser nobility and gentry for commemorative purposes such as weddings and christenings [figures 50 and 60], and with tools of various trades for those engaged in them. The large and imposing *Reichsadlerhumpen* (Imperial Eagle tankard) appears in figure 106, and an expanded version from Hanover's

49 Pilgrim-bottle enamelled with Coats of Arms in the Venetian manner. South German. Second half of the sixteenth century. The Arms are those of Wilhelm von Rappolstein of Alsace and of the first Count Liechtenstein, who married von Rappolstein's daughter

50 'Family' or 'Household' beaker, decorated in enamel colours and used for communal drinking. German. 1695

51 German glass. *(left to right)* Small bowl of yellowish-green metal (*Waldglas*), fourteenth to fifteenth century; *Krautstrunk* glass, bluish-green metal, sixteenth century; beaker of thick brownish-green glass, seventeenth century

52 *Hausmalerei*. An octagonal bottle painted in sepia, red and black. Attributed to Hermann Benckertt of Nürnberg. *c.* 1680

53 *Hausmalerei*. Tumbler painted with a landscape in *Schwarzlot* by Johann Schaper of Nürnberg. *c.* 1665

Kestner Museum showing the Arms usually encircling it in figure 103. Less handsomely decorated are the *Kurfürstenhumpen* (bearing the arms of the Electors) and the *Apostelgläser*, depicting the twelve Apostles. Centres of enamelling were widespread throughout Germany, Bohemia, and Austria, the earliest being established in the forests of Bavaria and the latest in Brandenburg. Perhaps the finest glasses of this kind came from Saxony.

The German love of painted decoration also found expression in *Kalte Malerei* (cold painting), often combined with gilding and sometimes with diamond-engraving. These glasses appear to have come principally from Nürnberg and Hall (Tirol). Some are painted on a gold or silver ground with oil colours, usually now in a worn condition, or even in colours suspended in a lacquer medium, similar to those employed by Martin Schnell to decorate the glazed stoneware of Böttger at Meissen.

Shortly before the middle of the seventeenth century a new departure occurs in the emergence of the *Hausmaler* (home painter), who enamelled independently on glass, faience, and, in rare instances, on Chinese porcelain, firing his work in a small enamelling-kiln at home. These men were responsible for some of the most sought-after work of the period. For the most part they worked in South Germany, at Augsburg and Nürnberg, and the first of them, Johann Schaper (1621–1670), painted chiefly in *Schwarzlot*, a black enamel used predominantly in a linear style suggested by engravings. Schaper, who had been a maker of stained-glass windows, scratched his designs with a sharp point through a black enamel ground, in addition to normal brushwork, and some specimens of his work have slight passages of red as well as gilding. A few examples entirely in red monochrome are known.

The work of Schaper and his followers is of a quality not hitherto to be seen in glass-painting, and J. L. Faber, who used the *Schwarzlot* technique, perhaps introduced translucent enamels, which are different from the colours employed by the earlier enamellers of German glass which were opacified, probably with tin-oxide, a substance in common use among the German makers of faience stove tiles. The Nürnberger, Abraham Helmhack (1654–1724), made more extensive use of coloured enamels, as well as a purple monochrome, and Honey *(Glass)* draws attention to a circular lantern-slide painted by Helmhack in unfired pigment for the newly-invented lantern of Kircher. Daniel Preuss-

54 Long-necked Syrian bottle decorated with Chinese *motifs* and an inscription in Kufic lettering in praise of an unknown sultan. End of the thirteenth century

55 Chinese vase of 'cased' glass carved in the manner of jade. Eighteenth century

ler of Silesia, and his son, Ignaz, worked on glass made locally, particularly in grey (en grisaille) and in black monochrome, painting especially mythological and hunting-scenes in a baroque style [figure 56].

Diamond-engraving in Germany began soon after the middle of the sixteenth century, inspired by similar work in Venice. Some work of this kind, done at Hall [figure 61], was on glass of a Venetian type, but this was not especially suitable for engraving, and the German love of enamelling was probably responsible for the technique remaining un-fashionable. Peter Wolff of Cologne engraved and signed some *Römer* in this way about 1670. A much later amateur glass-engraver, better known to lovers of old German por-celain, was the Canon August Otto Ernst von dem Busch (1704–1779) of Hildesheim, who drew landscapes, figures, floral subjects, and animals on glass and porcelain, filling the incised lines with black pigment.

Engraving with copper or bronze wheels, of the kind practised in Rome and by the German cutters of the much-loved *Bergkristall* (rock-crystal), was first done on glass towards the end of the sixteenth century. The earliest and best known of these cutters, Caspar Lehmann, worked in Prague for Rudolf II, and an example of his work is dated 1605 [figure 59].

Wheel-engraving was often done *intaglio*, that is the decoration is below the original surface. This is the German *Tiefschnitt* (deep-cutting), and in effect it resembles the *intaglio* gems of the ancients. Relief carving was some-times shallow and barely perceptible, but a much higher relief *(Hochschnitt)*, resembling the ancient cameo-cutting, was employed for the finest engraved glass. Work of this kind was always influenced by rock-crystal carving, an example of which is shown in figure 63 for comparison.

It is, perhaps, not surprising that wheel-engraving devel-oped slowly, and probably with many breakages. Apart from the work of the Roman *diatretarii*, wheel-engraving did not become a popular method of decoration until the seventeenth century was well advanced, and one of the reasons for the change was the availability of potash glass, which had its origin in the earlier *Waldglas*. For this, wood-ash had provided the source of alkali, and towards the end of the seventeenth century the Bohemian glass-makers improved it with the addition of extra lime, which gave a metal more tolerant of cutting and with a more brilliant surface than the soda-lime variety.

56 *Hausmalerei*. Armorial goblet painted by Ignaz Preussler with a coat of arms. On the foot, a view of Breslau. *c.* 1700

57 A beaker diamond-engraved with the Holy Roman Emperor, Rudolf II and the Electors with their arms. Dated 1594

58 A beaker enamelled in colours with the same subject. South German. Dated 1592

59 Pane. *Perseus and Andromeda*, in matt engraving. By Caspar Lehmann. 1605

The monopoly earlier granted to Lehmann was transferred at his death to a pupil, Georg Schwanhardt of Nürnberg (1601–1667), who worked also in rock-crystal. Schwanhardt's technique, on the basis of a few surviving signed pieces, was a mixture of wheel and diamond-engraving, and he also polished some of the broadly-cut surfaces which had hitherto been allowed to remain matt (i.e. with a dull or frosted appearance). This practice of contrasting matt and polished engraving in the same work contributed to the development of an increasingly pictorial style of decoration [figure 68].

Schwanhardt had two sons, Georg and Heinrich, who were also skilled engravers, and Doppelmayr, writing in 1730, refers to a method of glass-etching said to have been devised by Heinrich. This sounds unlikely, but a specimen probably done in this way is in the collection of the Germanisches Museum at Nürnberg, and is dated 1686.

Three pupils, followers of the Schwanhardts, did similar engraved work, bringing the art into the eighteenth century, although there is little evidence of Nürnberg engraving thereafter. These were Hermann Schwinger

60 Montage of figure 50, showing the decoration. The following is a translation of the verse:

Blessed by the Holy Trinity
Be he who drinks me dry –
We expect God and good luck
Every minute of the day.
Anno Do: 1695

(d. 1683), H. W. Schmidt (active 1690–5), and Georg Friedrich Killinger (d. 1726). The Nürnberg *Hausmaler* and goldsmith, Johann Heel (1637–1709), who painted faience and who may have mounted in metal some of Schaper's faience painting, probably engraved glass also, particularly some rare specimens of ruby-glass, a type later discussed.

Bohemia and Silesia gave a home to many glass-engravers from the middle of the seventeenth century onwards, and the numerous mountain streams of the Riesengebirge provided motive-power for the wheels and for polishing the finished work. Friedrich Winter worked at Petersdorff making goblets carved in the high-relief technique (*Hochschnitt*) from about 1690 onwards [figure 65]. Specimens of his work are now exceedingly rare. He used a heavy glass, in form related to contemporary silver. But the metal of the glass of this period was not as good as the decoration, and it sometimes shows a degree of degeneration which suggests that the process of adding lime to potash-glass had not yet been fully mastered.

Friedrich Winter's brother, Martin, was able to start a workshop at Potsdam with the aid of the Great Elector, Friedrich Wilhelm of Brandenburg; there he and his nephew, Gottfried Spiller, did some notable work in both *Hochschnitt* and *Tiefschnitt*. This was the time of the late baroque style, familiar in the decoration of early Meissen porcelain, and in the silver of Dinglinger at Dresden and of the Nürnberg and Augsburg craftsmen, who, like the glass-engravers, drew inspiration from books of ornament produced especially for the purpose by such designers as Paul Decker, Johann Eysler, and J. C. Reiff, which were

61 A diamond-engraved vase-shaped goblet and cover decorated with arabesques in the Venetian manner. Hall im Tirol. *c.* 1580

51

published by J. C. Weigel of Nürnberg at the beginning of the eighteenth century. These provided variations on such baroque themes as the *Laub- und Bandelwerk* (leaf and strap-work) which commonly appear on every kind of German and Austrian decorative art of the period [figure 48].

Potsdam continued to be famed for its engraving throughout the first half of the eighteenth century, but engraving is not the only decorative process for which it was noted. The glass-house established here under the patronage of the Great Elector in 1679 had for its Director the chemist, Johann Kunckel, who had published a treatise dealing with glass manufacture, the *Ars Vitraria Experimentalis*.

Sometime before 1679, Andreas Cassius of Leyden discovered that gold chloride used as a pigment yielded a fine rose-pink in favourable circumstances, although the colour sometimes varied in the direction of violet or purple, especially when mixed with tin-oxide and used for decorating pottery and porcelain. This pigment is remarkable not only for its popularity, but for the rapidity with which knowledge of its constitution spread far and wide.

Gold chloride was the colouring agent of the rich ruby-red glass devised by Kunckel about 1679, and apart from the ruby-glass of Heel which may have been a separate discovery, the colour can be regarded as a Potsdam speciality. Technically this pigment is not difficult to use, and the 'reducing' firing essential to the development of copper-red is not required. It is, however, necessary to cool ruby-glass coloured with gold very slowly. Rapid cooling prevents the colour from developing. The effect is much more uniform than that of copper, and the shade is under greater control. Knowledge of the colour to be derived from gold chloride appears to have become common property very soon after its discovery, and there is no reason why Heel, as well as Kunckel, should not have experimented with it at the same time.

Also from Potsdam came an opaque white glass, often called *Milchglas*, but sometimes (much more significantly) *Porcelleinglas*, and this was made at the same time as the making of porcelain in Germany was in the early stages of its development. A factory at Basdorf also produced white glass enamelled in the manner of porcelain towards the middle of the eighteenth century. Blue glass from Potsdam is usually thick, which suggests that the factory experienced trouble in using cobalt oxide for colouring thin

63 For comparison: goblet (*Pokal*) of rock-crystal (*Bergkristall*) carved with a hunting scene in the Court Workshop. Prague. *c.* 1625

64 Large covered *Römer* with decoration emblematic of the Four Elements, in matt and polished engraving. South German. *c.* 1735

65 A Petersdorff *Pokal* wheel-engraved with a portrait of Augustus the Strong, Elector of Saxony. By Friedrich Winter. *c.* 1690

66 Jar and cover, wheel-engraved with a Bacchanalian scene by Gottfried Spiller. Potsdam. *c.* 1700

glass. It sometimes assumes an undesirable purple shade in these circumstances.

Among the more important German glass-engravers is Franz Gondelach, who worked for the Landgrave of Hessen-Cassel with the title of *Hofglasschneider* (Court Glass-cutter, from *schneiden* to cut or carve). Gondelach frequently used Potsdam glass, but Hesse became a noted centre for glass-manufacture in West Germany during the eighteenth century.

Silesia took the lead from Bohemia in the first decades of the eighteenth century, when the glass-engraving of the region was much sought-after outside the borders of Germany. In Silesia the asymmetrical rococo style became fashionable shortly before 1750, but the industry began to decay soon afterwards under pressure of competition from England. It was revived in Bohemia during the nineteenth century, when amber glass, and clear glass flashed with ruby and other colours, in the form of cups, goblets and vases, was deeply engraved with finely-detailed topographical scenes, hunting scenes, and the like. This is sometimes termed 'overlay' glass. A florid version of the neo-classical style was popular during the early decades, and during the second half of the nineteenth century some of the older techniques were revived in a degenerate form. Black glass in imitation of Wedgwood's basalt wares seems to have been made in this region.

67 Faceted beaker decorated with grotesques in the manner of the French Court-designer, Jean Bérain, in *Schwarzlot* and gilding. Silesia. *c.* 1720

53

68 *Pokal* (lacking cover) engraved with shipping scenes. Nürnberg. *c.* 1665

The grinding of glass into facets, analogous to the cutting of precious stones and done for much the same reason, is discussed later because it was primarily a fashion developed by English glass-makers, but work of this kind was also done in Germany, where the cutting is characteristic and not difficult to recognize.

At the end of the seventeenth century coloured hardstones were once again extremely fashionable. The researches of Ehrenfried Walther von Tschirnhaus, a Saxon nobleman, which led eventually to the discovery of the red stoneware and porcelain made at Meissen, were also directed towards the manufacture of artificial hardstones fused with the aid of large burning-mirrors, which focussed the rays of the sun to give an intense heat. Like the Alexandrians and the Venetians before them, the German glass-makers also sought ways of imitating the natural stones. A factory was built at Dresden in 1699 with the patronage of Augustus the Strong, Elector of Saxony and King of Poland, for the purpose of making glass and artificial agate, and a few years later, after the advent of the red stoneware, a *Schleif- und Poliermühle* (a grinding and polishing mill) was built for the purpose of engraving red stoneware and grinding it into facets with the aid of Bohemian glass-workers. The manufacture and decoration of glass was in this way connected with decorative hardstones on the one hand and with porcelain and stoneware on the other. Although specimens are now difficult to identify, the Dresden glass-houses produced a good deal of engraved work of excellent quality. 'Marbled' glass in imitation of hardstones was revived in Bohemia during the nineteenth century.

'Gold sandwich' glass was another ancient technique employed in a slightly different form during the early years of the eighteenth century. These, the *Zwischengoldgläser*, are in fact double glasses, one fitting exactly inside the other [figure 67]. Some are painted in oil-colour on the interior of the larger, the smaller being given a gold or silver ground *(Zwischensilbergläser)*. Fitted together, the rim was sealed with lacquer varnish and disguised with a gold band, and simple cutting of the exterior was common. There were a number of variations practised on this theme, however, some quite elaborate. That of Mildner may be taken as an example. He cut an oval recess into the surface of heavily-made beakers, some of which had handles and covers, and inserted medallions covering designs in silver,

69 *Pokal*, wheel-engraved, with the addition of cold painting and gilding. The portrait is of the Czarina Elizabeth of Russia. Hesse. *c.* 1750

70 'Thumb' glass (*Daumenglas*) so-called from the hemispherical indentions, which look as though made by the pressure of the thumb on soft metal. Probably Hesse (sixteenth to seventeenth century); with a pair of ring-glasses of the same period

gold and red lacquer. Much of his work was signed and dated. Most glass of this kind came from Bohemia, Silesia or Austria.

Related to this technique is *verre églomisé* [figure 135], a term thought to be derived from a French picture-frame maker of the eighteenth century named Glomy. Similar work was done by a Dutchman named Zeuner, working in Amsterdam, who applied silver and gold leaf to the underside of a sheet of glass and then engraved designs through it in a linear style, protecting his finished work with varnish or a layer of tin-foil. An example of his work in the Buckley Collection (Victoria and Albert Museum) is signed 'Zeuner' and dated 1773.

The art of the Rhineland has always differed from that of others parts of Germany. Roman civilization found a foothold here when the remainder of Germany was still forest, and the cage-cup [figure 12] is but one of the most remarkable discoveries from the Roman period which have been made in this region. The relationship between later Rhineland·glass and that made and decorated in the Netherlands is often close, and it is, therefore, convenient to consider them successively.

The early 'claw-beaker' was certainly made in· the Rhineland, and it is possible that most of the specimens which have been recovered in Europe came from this area

71 *Zwischengoldglas* ('gold sandwich') beaker decorated with a bear hunt. Bohemia. *c*. 1750

72 *Passglas*, the rings of trailed and indented glass. German. Sixteenth to seventeenth century

Descended from it is the *Igel*, the 'hedgehog' glass of the fifteenth century, the pointed drops of glass being exaggerately drawn out in sixteenth century specimens. The *Römer* (a name of uncertain derivation) was a very popular glass for hock [figure 77] and, like the *Igel*, it was usually made in a green metal. Its stem is decorated with glass drops, termed prunts, which in the seventeenth century were impressed with a pattern of raised dots somewhat resembling the surface of a raspberry, and often called the 'raspberry prunt'. The plain prunt drawn out to a blunt point also appears on glasses of this period. A few rare specimens have prunts in the form of a lion-mask, and these may perhaps be said to show Venetian influence, the mask being the lion of St Mark. The hollow stem of the early *Römer* was made by winding softened glass-rod in a spiral round a conical wooden former, the bowl being welded to it. The hollow blown foot is a trifle later, and, in the eighteenth century and after, the rod was wound over a blown stem, which serves to separate it from earlier work.

Usually from the Rhineland is the sixteenth-century cylindrical beaker, the *Passglas*, plain and encircled by a notched spiral thread, or by more or less equidistant threads, the base inside rising to a cone. These, like the English silver peg-tankards, were intended for communal drinking, the threads serving to mark the amount to be consumed by each person.

Reference has already been made to Altarist and Venetian influences on glass-making in the Netherlands, and the Italian manner persisted almost until the end of the seventeenth century. In consequence of the accession of William of Orange to the English throne the relationship between England and Holland became much closer, and cultural and technical interchanges between the two countries were common. In this way Dutch glass-makers began tentatively to imitate the lead-glass of the Englishman, Ravenscroft.

By 1680 the Bonhomme family, glass-makers of Liège, were imitating contemporary German work, and making small and experimental quantities of lead-glass with the aid of English workmen. Like German and English glass of the period, a certain amount of degeneration of the kind known as crisselling is to be observed in some of it. During the eighteenth century especially the Dutch were often decorators rather than manufacturers, in glass as well as in certain kinds of pottery, and this was probably due to a general shortage of wood as fuel in the Low Countries.

73 Persian ewer, in form based on contemporary metalwork, with gilded decoration. Reign of Shah Abbas (1585–1625)

74. *Basket of glasses* (1644) by the Strasbourg
painter Sebastien Stoskopff

For this reason much work from this part of Europe
has been executed on imported glasses.

A Netherlands speciality, perhaps originally taken from
the Rhineland, was diamond-engraving, which was continued into the nineteenth century, long after it had
become unpopular elsewhere. The art of engraving falls
into two distinct categories: wheel-engraving, commonly
practised in Bohemia and Silesia, but, with the exception of
Jacob Sang of Amsterdam, little used in the Netherlands,
and diamond-engraving which was the rule.

That the technique came to the Netherlands at an early
date is proved by the existence of a beaker in a Dutch collection dated 1581, and another dated 1590 is in the Rijks-
museum at Amsterdam. Engraving during the first half of
the seventeenth century was in the Venetian manner, and
the best known of the early engravers was Anna Roemers
Visscher (1583–1651), from whose hand several dated
examples have survived in Germany and Holland. Her
sister, Maria Tesselschade Roemers Visscher (1594–1649),
and another woman, Anna Maria von Schurmann (1607–

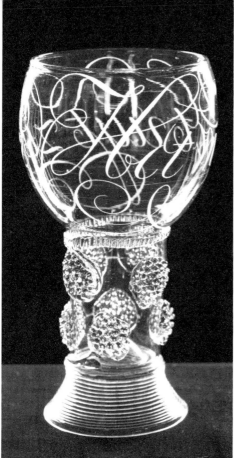

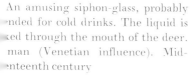
An amusing siphon-glass, probably
intended for cold drinks. The liquid is
sucked through the mouth of the deer.
German (Venetian influence). Mid-
seventeenth century

76 *Römer* with spirally-wound foot
and calligraphic engraving, probably
by Anna Roemers Visscher. Towards
1650

77 *Römer*, spirally-wound foot and raspberry
prunts. Decorated with the Arms of Holland,
those of William III and Mary, and of the
Seven Provinces. Dated 19 April 1689

1678), did work in a similar style. Willem Jacobz van
Heemskerk (1613–1692) of Leyden also signed and dated
several glasses. Like Canon Busch most of these engravers
were amateurs who were noted in other fields.

The glasses of Anna Roemers Visscher were often engraved with well-observed flowers, fruit, and the like, taken
from contemporary prints, with encircling borders and inscriptions in the Greek and Latin alphabets. Her style is
linear and calligraphic [figure 76], with a certain amount
of cross-hatching. On one glass, however, she used stippling instead of cross-hatching, a process which was to become exclusively a Dutch preserve. Stippling was executed
with a diamond-pointed instrument tapped with a light
hammer with sufficient force to mark the surface. The decoration was built up from these dots, which were widely or
closely spaced according to the demands of the pattern.

Referring to the work of an amateur, Frans Green-

wood (1680–1761), who first developed the technique of stippling, a contemporary, J. van Gool, likened the effect to drawing with white chalk on coloured paper, the stippled parts providing the high-lights and the clear glass the shadows. So laborious was this work that it was suitable only as a pastime; no one could do it profitably [figure 81].

Greenwood started as a diamond-engraver [figure 80]. The stippling technique may have been suggested to him by the newly-fashionable art of engraving in *mezzotinto* invented by Ludwig von Siegen of Utrecht in 1643. The punch-engraving of copper-plates for printing by Jan Lutma the Younger has also been regarded as influential, but it seems much more likely that stippling evolved from the goldsmith's use of the dotting-punch in conjunction with line-engraving in the decoration of metalwork. What-ever the origin stippling became extremely popular as a method of decorating glass during the eighteenth century, and some signed and dated work, inferior in quality to that of Greenwood, came from David Wolff (1732–1798) towards the end of the eighteenth century [figure 83].

Most work in diamond-engraving or stippling is based

80 English goblet line-engraved in Holland by Frans Greenwood with Italian Comedy figures based on the work of Callot. Signed, dated 1720

81 English goblet stippled with the portrait of a man holding a *Römer*, by Frans Greenwood. Signed, dated 1720

82 Goblet (perhaps English) stippled with a man dining, by Aert Schouman. Signed, dated 1751

on contemporary prints, some of which have been traced, and Aert Schouman (1720–1792), one of Greenwood's followers, was both a painter and an engraver in *mezzotinto* [figures 82 and 84]. Stipple-engraved glasses are not unusual today, but in the absence of a signature or a monogram, they are not easy to attribute. Dutch wheel-engraving, also, can be separated from German only with difficulty. Glass thus decorated dates from the last decades of the seventeenth century, and Jacob Sang of Amsterdam (active 1750 onwards) is the most widely-known engraver of this kind. Dutch work is much rarer than German.

The *latticino* technique of the Venetians was adapted in Holland to the decoration of those wine-glass stems which have opaque white spiral threads embedded in the clear glass, and these were copied in England by 1750 or very soon afterwards.

83 (*left*) Goblet with faceted stem, stippled by David Wolff. *c.* 1780

84 (*below left*) An example of Schouman's signature: *A Schouman Fec-1752*

85 Bowl of a wine-glass, perhaps stippled by David Wolff. The inscription reads '*Vriendschap*' (Friendship). *c.* 1780

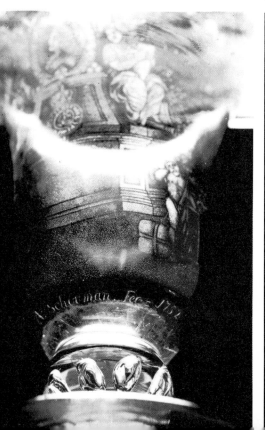

86 *(left) The Fairfax Cup.* This, enamelled with the story of Pyramus and Thisbe, was in the possession of the Fairfax family of Yarm, in Yorkshire, for centuries. Venetian glass. Fifteenth century

87 Venetian goblet enamelled with Italian Comedy figures. Early sixteenth century

France and Spain

88 A very rare enamelled glass chalice decorated with the Crucifixion, probably by immigrant Venetian workmen. France. Sixteenth century

THE EARLIEST FRENCH GLASS, of which rare specimens survive, has already been mentioned briefly, and glasshouses were established by Italian workmen in the fifteenth century, although little is known about them. Enamelling of good quality occurs during the sixteenth century [figure 88], some with French inscriptions. Glass 'splashed' with spots of enamel, related to similarly decorated faience from Nevers, can also be seen in the much later English glass from Nailsea, near Bristol.

Nothing is known for certain of diamond- or wheel-engraving in France. There are a few specimens of moulded glass made towards the end of the seventeenth century which may have been the work of Bernard Perrot, who also experimented with opaque white glass in the style of porcelain at Fay-aux-Loges near Orléans in the early years of the eighteenth century. Among the more important centres to be settled by Italian workmen may be numbered Nevers in the Loire valley, a fief of the Gonzaga family from Mantua since 1564, where faience in the Italian style was also made. Here some amusing glass figures were made 'at the lamp', of which a rare example probably from here appears in figure 89.

Mirrors of glass were attempted in France as early as the thirteenth century by Lorraine glass-workers, who used lead foil as a reflective backing. It is still undetermined whether or not mirrors were made before this date, but the balance of probability is in favour of a Roman origin. Several attempts were made later to revive the industry in France, but the problem did not become acute until the enormous cost of installing Venetian mirrors in the Galérie des Glaces at Versailles had to be faced. Colbert, the Finance Minister of Louis Quatorze, who was responsible for raising money to furnish the new palace, exerted himself strenuously to establish the industry in Paris, but two of his most skilled workmen imported from Venice died within a week or two of each other in mysterious circumstances.

Bernard Perrot was apparently responsible for the discovery which enabled glass to be cast in sheets, and this seems to have been what would now be described as plate-glass. There is little reliable information about the nature of his invention, but it may have included some kind of rolling in the modern manner. A factory was started in Picardy in 1693 to manufacture mirrors, which was then amalgamated with Colbert's original factory in the Faubourg St Antoine in Paris which had already transferred part of its manufacture to Normandy. What seems to be the only contemporary account of the Paris factory is given by Queen Anne's physician, Dr Martin Lister, in his *Journey to Paris*, published in 1698:

> The Glass-house out of the Gate of St Antoine well deserves seeing; but I did lament the Fondery was no longer there, but removed to Cherborne in Normandy for cheapness of Fuel. This is certainly a most considerable addition to the Glass-making. For I saw here one Looking-glass foiled and finished, 88 inches long and 48 inches broad; and yet but one quarter of an inch thick. This, I think, could never be effected by the Blast of any Man [a reference to the Lorraine process of sheet-glass making by blowing]; but I suppose to be run or cast upon sand, as Lead is; which yet, I confess, the toughness of Glass Metall makes very much against.
> There they are polished; which Imploys daily 600 Men, and they hope in a little time to employ a 1000 in several Galleries. In the lower they grind the course Glass with a Sand Stone, the very same they Pave the Streets in Paris; of which broken they have great heaps in the Courts of the Work-houses; This stone is beat to powder and sifted through a fine Tamis [straining-cloth]. In the Upper Gallery, where they polish and give the last Hand, they work in 3 Rowes, and 2 Men at a Plate, with Ruddle or Powdered Haematites in Water.
> The Glasses are set fast in White Puttie, upon flat Tables of Stone, sawed thin for that purpose. The grinding the Edges and Borders is very troublesome, and odious for the horrid grating noise it makes, and which cannot be endured to one not used to it; and yet by long custom these Fellows are so easie with it, that they Discourse together as nothing were. This is done below, and out of the way of the rest ... [It] has made Glass for Coaches very cheap and common ...

89 A glass figure worked 'at the lamp' Nevers. Seventeenth century

It is a little surprising that the craftsmen of France, highly skilled in most other fields, should have lagged behind in the craft of decorative glass-making, preferring that requirements be imported from England, Germany, and Italy. The Baccarat factory was not established until 1765, where English glass was at first extensively imitated [figure 127], and other factories were started for a similar purpose towards the end of the eighteenth century. Some remarkably fine work, much more in the French tradition, was done towards the end of the nineteenth century and later, especially that of Emile Gallé and René Lalique, who worked in the *art nouveau* style.

Little is known of glass-making in Spain before the sixteenth century when Andalusian, Catalonian, and Castilian glass-works freely imitated Venetian styles and techniques. Enamelling was done at Barcelona and elsewhere, with the addition of cold (unfired) gilding during the six-

90 *(left)* Venetian plate of opaque white glass enamelled in the manner of porcelain with a view of San Giorgio Maggiore. *c.* 1740

91 Ringed goblet decorated in *Schwarzlot* with scenes celebrating the Baptism of the Elector of Bavaria, Max Emmanuel. 1662

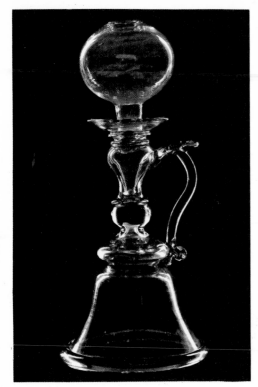

92 A lace-maker's lamp. France. c. 1760

93 A mirror to which silver foil or paper printed in sepia has been applied, the back protected with a further addition of lead. The subject is St Francis of Sales. France. Late seventeenth century

94 *Cántaro* (water-vessel) with *latticino* decoration in the Venetian manner. Spain. Eighteenth century

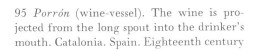

95 *Porrón* (wine-vessel). The wine is projected from the long spout into the drinker's mouth. Catalonia. Spain. Eighteenth century

96 *(above)* An Andalusian vase with many handles. There are perhaps lingering traces of Moorish influence, especially in the form of the vase. Spain. Late sixteenth century

97 and 98 Two *almorratas* (rose-water sprinklers). Seventeenth century. *(left)* From Catalonia. *(right)* From Venice, of more accomplished workmanship. The bosses are moulded with the lion-head of St Mark

99 Shaped dish engraved with formal flowers. La Granja de San Ildefonso. Spain. *c.* 1765

100 Glasses and bottles being removed from the furnaces and carried to the shops in baskets. From the *Grande Encyclopédie*

teenth century. Ice-glass in the Venetian manner occurs towards the end of this century, and occasional diamond-point engraving begins soon after it.

Most Spanish glass depends for its form on the skill of the glass-blower. Although Venetian influence is strong most vessels are characteristically Spanish. The *cántaro* is a curiously-shaped water-vessel with a ring-handle at the top, usually with a bird or flower-shaped finial and a double spout [figure 94]; the *porrón*, a flat-based wine-vessel with a long spout from which, when held above the head, the wine could be projected in a stream, as though from a goat-skin [figure 95]; and the *almorrata*, a rose-water sprinkler with a large neck and four small sprinkler-spouts, shown in Venetian and Spanish forms in figures 97 and 98. *Latticino* decoration sometimes occurs, with much freely added ornament of trailed glass worked with pincers and other tools.

In the eighteenth century a variety of mugs, drinking-glasses, vases, urns, and decorative items of all kinds were made in Catalonia, vases especially being ornamented with pincered glass. Wheel-engraving was started in the first half of the eighteenth century by Laurence Eder, of Swedish origin, and others who worked in the Bohemian style at the Royal factory of La Granja de San Ildefonso, founded in 1728. The nature of Spanish glass, however, made it inferior material for this kind of work [figure 99]. Despite financial stringencies experienced at mid-century the Royal factory continued to experiment with a large number of processes, especially those contained in a book written by Antonio Neri, *L'arte vetraria*, published in Florence in 1612, and in the work of Kunckel already mentioned.

Opaque white glass summarily enamelled was probably intended to compete with porcelain, and porcelain painters from the Royal factory of Buen Retiro at Madrid were also employed at the glass-house. Decoration in gold, introduced by Sigismund Brun, was commonly used, sometimes in conjunction with wheel-engraving. This was 'honey-gold', gold ground up in honey and fixed with a light firing, similar to that used by the porcelain factories of Sèvres and Chelsea.

Spanish glass-workers were especially adept in assembling chandeliers from cut-glass pendant drops.

English, Irish and American glass

THE SMALL Sussex town of Chiddingfold was once an important centre of glass-making in England, and the remains of glass-houses dating from the thirteenth century have been found during excavation. Bracken and beech-wood ash provided the alkali, and blowing was the principal method of manufacture. Window-glass was made here in the fourteenth century according to surviving records, and the workmen all seem to have come from the Continent. One, John le Alemayn, was obviously German, probably from the Rhineland.

About the middle of the sixteenth century glass-workers from Lorraine established themselves near Alfold in Surrey, and shortly afterwards they were in London. They imported their soda in the form of *barilla* from Alicante in Spain, a source also drawn upon by the Venetians. *Barilla*, obtained from burning a plant growing in salt-marshes, described at the time as 'a strange kind of vegetable – a thick earthy shrub bearing berries like barberries', contained both lime and soda and it was eminently suited for making 'cristal'. A large export trade in this ash grew up between Spain and those parts of glass-making Europe which were within reach of the sea.

The immigrants sought monopolies for their craft. One such concession in 1567 speaks of the 'art, feate, or mystery of making glas such as is made in Fraunce, Lorayne and Burgondy, and was given in exchange for a share of the profits. These monopolies, which were sparingly granted, required that Englishmen be taught the necessary skills, a condition, like the payment of the money due, not generally fulfilled.

The many disputes caused the Lorraine glass-makers to remove themselves to the Midlands, especially to the area around Stourbridge which became a notable glass-making centre, and a few penetrated as far north as Newcastle-on-Tyne. In 1615 an edict forbade the use of wood as fuel, but by this time nearly all glass-makers had adapted their furnaces to pit-coal instead of charcoal. Those of Antwerp and Liège had already probably changed to coal, although the porcelain-makers of France especially did not come to it until late in the eighteenth century, when those of Lille fired their kilns with coal.

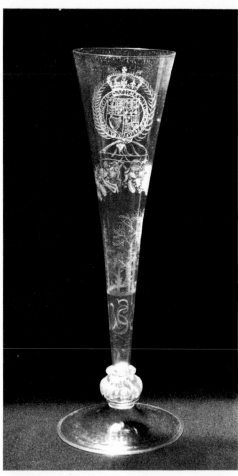

The Venetian, Verzelini, established his London glass-house in 1573, first at Crutched Friars and then in Austin Friars. The last-named factory later passed to the financier, Vice-Admiral Sir Robert Mansell, who made glass from Spanish *barilla* with the aid of pit-coal. Mansell secured the existing monopolies which gave him virtual control over glass-making in England, and with the aid of Altarist workmen he set up glass-houses throughout the country which supplied domestic needs of all kinds. Venetian, and Continental glass generally, was not only liable to duty, but it could only be imported under licence.

There is little surviving today which can be regarded as the work of Mansell's glass-houses, and it is not even certain what happened to his monopoly during the Civil War and the following Commonwealth. When, at the Restoration in 1660, the 'intolerant boor' was replaced by the 'genial blackguard' in the person of Charles II the decorative arts took a new lease of life. In 1663 George Villiers, Duke of Buckingham, petitioned the King for what may have been a renewal of Mansell's patent, although the technical knowledge was now provided by a Frenchman, John le Cam. Manufacture was directed towards an imitation of rock-crystal, which suggests a thicker metal, and of mirrors (or looking-glasses) for which a glass-house was set up in Vauxhall. Prices for looking-glasses fell, and on December 16th 1664 Pepys records that he 'bought a looking-glass by the Old Exchange which costs me £5. 5s and 6s. for the hooks. A very fair glass.'

The trade in glass from Venice was renewed at the same time, and correspondence between the Murano glass-maker, Alessio Morelli, and the London glass-importer, John Greene, warden of the Glass-Sellers' Company in 1677, enables us to reconstruct not only the kind of vessels being imported, but those fashionable with English makers also. The letters, with many drawings of the glasses ordered [figure 104], are preserved in the British Museum (Sloane Mss).

Few specimens of the actual glasses imported by Greene have survived, but they are of heavier metal than those Venetian glasses made for home-consumption because they had to withstand the hazards of transport, and perhaps for the same reason the stems were short. An unusual siphon glass which appears in Greene's drawings represents a type illustrated here by figure 75.

Greene was very definite as to the kind of glass he pre-

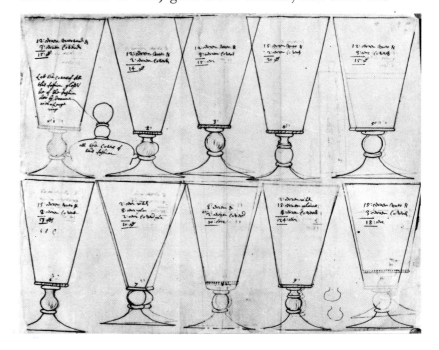

103 *(right)* Bohemian tankard. 1594. Montage, showing the whole of the Arms at a glance. Dated 1659

101 *(opposite, top) The Scudamore Flute.* Engraved with the Royal Arms and those of John, first Viscount Scudamore. Netherlandish in style. Probably engraved about 1665

102 *(opposite, bottom)* Goblet, the stem with a hollow knop, the bowl engraved with the Arms of Queen Elizabeth I, 'John . . . Jone', and 'Dier 1581', Probably made by Verzelini, and perhaps the work of a French engraver, Anthony de Lysle (or Lisley). The earliest known example of this kind is dated 1577

ferred, demanding in 1669 that 'all drinking glasses be well made of verij bright clear and whit(e) sound mettall, and as exactly as possible may bee to the formes'. Earlier he had said 'the fashions . . . we leave to you, onely Lett them be all with feet and most with ears'. In 1671 he asks to be used 'verij kindely in the prices . . . for we make now very good Drinking glasses in England', and in 1672 he complains that 'the last you sent the Mettall was indifferent good and clear, and not so sound or strong as they should have bin made', concluding 'I praij take much care that these be made of verij good sound Mettall, and thick and

104 *(right)* Drawings of glasses by John Greene enclosed in a letter to the Murano glass-maker Alessio Morelli

stronger than the last that I may gain Creditt by this though not so much proffitt'. The last remark seems to have been prompted by the system of Customs duties, and earlier he makes proposals for evading these by a new system of packing.

The next development of importance came in 1674 when Ravenscroft petitioned the King for a patent to make glass resembling rock-crystal in a new way. This was granted because Ravenscroft's formula differed from those of existing glass-houses, an 'escape' clause of this kind always forming part of every patent or monopoly. The first glass made by Ravenscroft was excessively liable to the defect of crisselling, although a report to the Glass-Sellers' Company of 1676 states that the defect had been overcome 'several

105 Bowl of crisselled glass, probably by Ravenscroft. London. c. 1675

months agoe'. That this was a premature conclusion is evidence that the degeneration was at first rapid and later took much longer to reveal itself. Crisselling is to be observed in glass made after the date quoted.

Ravenscroft first introduced lead into his metal about 1676, producing what came to be known as English 'flint' glass. Lead was usually added in the form of red lead, and

106 A *Reichsadlerhumpen* (Imperial eagle tankard) bearing the Arms of the Holy Roman Empire and the Electors

107 Detail of Ravenscroft's seal of the raven's head

the effect of its addition was to increase the weight and density of the metal, as well as its power of refraction, and to darken the colour.

Ravenscroft gave his new metal the seal of a raven's head [figure 107], of which a mere handful of specimens remain, and lead-glass was soon being widely manufactured, progressively darkening in colour as greater quantities of lead and manganese decolourizer were added. The Italian styles, unsuited to the new metal, were gradually abandoned, although the application of Venetian manipulative techniques to lead-glass may be noted in certain rare specimens belonging to the end of the seventeenth century and the first decade or so of the eighteenth, probably made by Italian or Dutch workmen [figure 112] English glass was now being exported in ever greater quantities to the Continent, where it was in demand for engraving [figures 81 and 82].

When, in 1713, George I succeeded to the English throne German fashions came with him. Until the accession of Queen Victoria in 1837 English sovereigns were also Electors of Hanover, a title which passed to the Duke of Cumberland in that year. As early as the reign of Dutch William and Queen Mary some mediocre commemorative engraving done in Holland is to be noticed, and 'Williamite' glasses commemorating the Battle of the Boyne persisted among the Orangemen of Northern Ireland, engraved in Holland from about 1740 onwards.

As a result of these new influences engraved work in England improved in quality and increased in quantity, although a fairly distinctive English flavour is the rule. Glass exported from Newcastle to the Netherlands was engraved to appeal to the Continental market, although some rare examples of English subjects may have been executed in Holland for this country.

Engraved glasses, English and Continental, often commemorate in their design all kinds of events and persons of note. Portraits of kings, statesmen, and soldiers are usually easy to date within a year or two. As an example, the appearance of Frederick the Great on English glass or porcelain denotes some time during the early stages of the Seven Years' War, probably 1757, when he was at the height of his popularity in England. Peace-treaties, battles, and all such events are not difficult to place in their period, since they would hardly have been commemorated in this way after they had passed into history. The more prosaic

108 Jug of characteristic style by Ravenscroft. London. c. 1675

emblems of trades and professions, the symbols of Freemasonry and glasses made for clubs and regiments, are all to be found, and a variety with a perennial interest for the collector comprises the very rare 'Jacobite' glasses.

Most of these belong to the middle of the eighteenth century, when Jacobite societies which supported the Stuart cause proliferated, especially in the Border counties of England. The designs are usually symbolic and the meaning obscure and controversial. Apart from portraits and inscriptions, which can hardly be misunderstood, Jacobite glasses are commonly engraved with the oak-leaf (a refer-

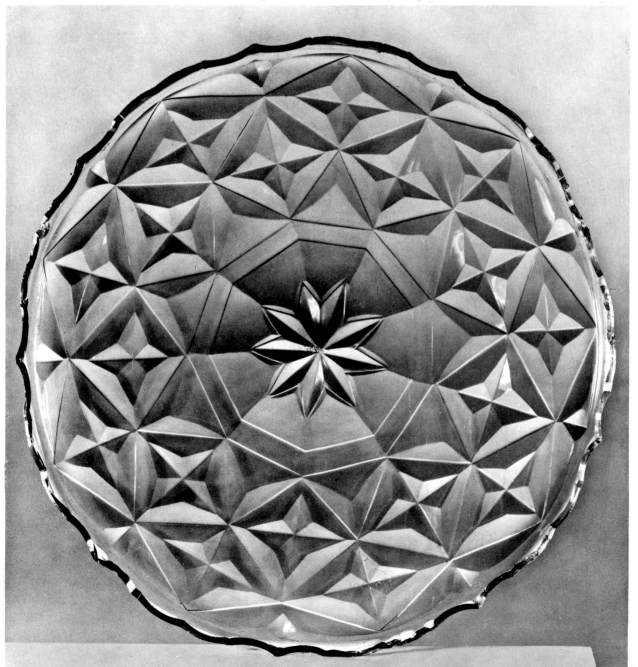

109 A circular Irish tray (*c.* 1800) showing clearly the principles of good facet-cutting

110 Pilgrim-bottle of green glass, mounted in ormolu, probably at Augsburg. German. Seventeenth century

ence to the Boscobel oak), roses with one or two buds, the thistle of Scotland, and the word *Fiat* (Let it be) which was probably a motto of the Cycle Club, so-called because the members met in each other's houses. Most such glasses were made in Newcastle-on-Tyne and engraved (portrait glasses especially) in Edinburgh. Figure 113 shows a *Fiat* glass which also bears a wheel-like symbol. A seventeenth century reference to this symbol among the papers of John Greene (British Museum, Sloane Mss) describes this as meaning that God created Adam, the focus, by taking parts from all places, all virtues, all living, moving, fixed and unfixed creatures, with the word *Fiat*. In the Jacobite glasses the focus is obviously intended to be the Pretender, who was to be created king by a similar process.

The wine-glass shown in figure 114 is inscribed *Audentior Ibo*, sometimes thought to mean 'I will go more boldly next time'. This, however, is dog-latin so grammatically obscure that it seems more likely to be an error, and that it was wrongly copied by the engraver in the first place. *Audentior Bibo* (perhaps the correct reading) means 'I drink boldly'. The other rare glasses with the same tag

111 Three Jacobite glasses engraved with roses, and an oak-leaf growing, curiously enough, from a rose-stem. English. *c.* 1750

were probably engraved at the same time and copied from the first one. Errors of this kind are well-known on pottery and porcelain, the inscriptions being copied without understanding by illiterate painters.

Wine and sweetmeat-glasses with baluster stems date from the second half of the seventeenth century, although most belong to the eighteenth. The form was based to some extent on the architectural baluster, but many such baluster stems, and some of the knopped stems related to them, are distinctly reminiscent of the turned legs popular as supports for furniture of the period. After 1720 baluster stems became progressively lighter and smaller, but they did not disappear entirely until after mid-century. About 1715 there appeared a heavy ribbed and shouldered stem which is often called 'Silesian', although this term is strictly incorrect [figure 115]. The stem was, nevertheless, of German origin.

The early foot was more or less flat, but a domed foot, the rim sometimes folded over in the Venetian manner, is to be observed during the early years of the eighteenth century. Bowl, stem, and foot were made in three or four parts and welded together, and in the centre, under the foot, will be found a roughened patch of glass where it was joined originally during the course of manufacture to the pontil, an iron rod used to hold the embryo foot while it was being fashioned. This pontil-mark is very commonly present, although it has sometimes been ground smooth when a glass has been decoratively engraved or cut.

The earliest bowls were given the shape of a straight-sided funnel, and a tendency to curve does not become noticeable until the reign of George I, when thistle-shaped and ogee bowls were popular. Limited use continued to be made of the funnel which, as the century advanced, was drawn out and given slightly curving sides. A small straight-sided funnel with a flat bottom is termed a 'bucket'. The diameter of the bowl in early wine-glasses is rarely as great as that of the foot, and never exceeds it. Some extremely strong specimens with a short stem and a thick foot are termed 'firing-glasses', and were hammered on the table during popular toasts.

Noteworthy changes in the form of the stem begin to appear from about 1725 onwards, and baluster stems were sometimes ornamented with a single large air-bubble trapped in the interior. Until then it had been the practice to disguise air-bubbles wherever possible. Now they were deli-

112 English covered goblet in the Venetian style. Late seventeenth century

113 Wine-glass with air-twist stem engraved with the word *Fiat*, and the wheel symbol. English. *c.* 1745

114 Jacobite glass, the stem with an external twist, engraved with a portrait of Bonnie Prince Charlie, and an inscription, *Audentior Ibo. c.* 1745

115 Sweetmeat glass with a Silesian stem. Domed and folded foot. English. *c.* 1715

berately introduced by pricking a hole in the softened glass, which was then closed and drawn out a little so that the bubble became pear-shaped, with the point downwards.

Air-twists, introduced about 1745, are long spiral cavities running the whole length of the necessarily straight stem which replaced the baluster. At first a number of holes were pierced and closed in a large blob of glass formed at the base of the bowl, which was then drawn out and twisted until it became a straight rod enclosing spiral air-channels, and to this the foot was welded. Later, the stems were made separately and welded to bowl and foot.

Although it has been thought that the air-twist may have come before the enamel-twist, this is uncertain. White and coloured twists were more difficult to make than air-twists, necessitating a number of lengths of enamel thread being arranged in a tubular mould which was then filled with clear glass. Removed from this mould the stem was reheated and dexterously drawn out and twisted. At first simple, the twists became more complex towards the end of the eighteenth century, enamel tapes being combined with the threads, and mixed air and enamel-twists belong to the same period. By far the greater number of twists was made in England, but a small quantity came from Holland.

Cut-glass was a technique in which English glass-workers especially excelled during the eighteenth century. Facet-cutting, however, was rarely popular abroad as the sole means of decoration, although it was often employed as

117 *Hausmalerei*. Tumbler enamelled in red. Nürnberg. Late seventeenth century

118 Mirror in the form of a candle-sconce, with shallow bevels and wheel-engraved decoration. English. *c.* 1700

116 (*left*) *Hausmalerei*. Tumbler painted with polychrome enamels. Bohemia. *c.* 1730

ancillary ornament.

Cutting is carried out with revolving wheels of abrasive stone, or with iron wheels fed with sand and water, followed by polishing with wooden wheels charged with putty powder (tin oxide). Pliny clearly separates the revolving wheels from the gravers of the cameo-cutters, and some work of this kind had already been done in Germany. The beaker illustrated in figure 62, for instance, has been ground into simple facets. It was not until English glassmakers, in difficulty with their fuel supply, sought a metal which would fuse at a relatively low temperature and ex-

119 Table candlestick for four lights. English. London. *c.* 1700

120 A rare pair of candlesticks with air-twist decoration. English. *c.* 1750

perimented with lead as a flux, that glass well-adapted to cutting was produced. Nevertheless, singularly little use was made of it for this purpose until the eighteenth century was fairly well advanced, and the finest English work occurs between mid-century and the end of the Regency period in 1820.

Facet-cutting or grinding, as distinct from wheel-engraving, probably began in England with the makers of looking-glasses. It was the custom to buy rough plates from the glasses-houses, the finishing and foiling being done by those who carved the frames, and for this they needed abrasive wheels to cut the wide, shallow bevels which were then the rule. One maker of mirrors, James Welch of 'Black Fryers' in London, advertised himself in 1724 as 'Glass-grinder and Looking-glass Maker', and so great was the cost that, according to Symons, a system of weekly payments was introduced. Figure 118 shows a small mirror of the early years of the eighteenth century adapted as a candle-sconce, in which the shallow bevels and floral and geometric engraving are used as an effective decoration. In form it is not unlike contemporary silver sconces.

The first such cutting to vessels appears to have been done to the rims of sweetmeat glasses, and there are several references to 'scollopt' rims before 1740, perhaps with faceted stems also to be found on wine-glasses [figure 56]. This speedily evolved into much more elaborate slicing and faceting. The heyday of sliced cutting was in the 1770s, when particularly brilliant effects were obtained. Early cutting into pyramidal diamond-shapes was elaborated by grinding down the pyramid to a flat table, followed by cutting of the top at a right-angle to the sides ('strawberry diamond' and 'hobnail' cutting), especially to be seen in nineteenth century glass presumed to have been made in Ireland before 1825.

Chandeliers with cut-glass drops depending from grace-fully curving arms of glass, themselves elaborately faceted, were suggested by those of Versailles, where the arms were of brass and the drops shallow-cut. The fashion reached England by the mid-eighteenth century [figure 122]. At first intended for suspension, such chandeliers developed into handsome table ornaments after 1775, often with bases of Wedgwood's new jasper ware. Later specimens of English and Irish work made much use of deep prismatic cutting and multiple facets. Chandeliers are sometimes made up today from miscellaneous drops, and these composites

121 (*right*) A very fine cut-glass chandelier with pendant drops. English. London. *c.* 1770

122 Punch-bowl and cover of blown and tooled lead glass, the decoration wheel-engraved. English. Mid-eighteenth century

have been wittily described as a miniature history of glass during the past hundred and fifty years.

Some of the best cutting is to be found on salad-bowls and dessert dishes on high stands. Decanters also exhibit the prevailing fashions in cutting very well, beginning with a little light slicing and fluting which gave place, in turn, to a variety cut all over with shallow facets towards the end of the 1750s. These were replaced by more deeply cut facets in the 1760s when forms began to be more delicate and tapering. Engraving of flowers and foliage, neo-classical swags, stars, and long flutes in the neck belong to the 1770s. 'Diamond-cutting' began soon after 1790, but did not become popular until the early years of the nineteenth century, when deep cutting soon became the rule, especially on the shoulders. Stoppers, also, were cut in elegant patterns, the earlier circular and pear-shaped varieties giving way to a mushroom shape at the end of the eighteenth century, when they were fitted to a squat decanter heavily ornamented with cutting. Even more elaborately cut in diamonds were the large and imposing wine-coolers of the early nineteenth century which are now exceedingly rare.

A cautionary note is necessary for the benefit of the new collector of old cut-glass. Reproductions abound, made by pressing into moulds, although only the best are likely to

123 A very rare clock with a case of glass and ormolu. *c.* 1775

124 *Façon de Venise*. A Dutch goblet in the Venetian manner. Seventeenth century

be deceptive [figure 127]. Attempts to imitate the colour of old lead-glass are rarely very successful, but even more revealing is the appearance of the boundaries between the facets. In true cut-glass these are sharp and well-defined, a necessary effect of the method of manufacture. The edges of the facets of moulded glass, however, are blunt, both to sight and touch. The makers of these copies are aware of the defect, and ambitious reproductions have the more prominent moulded facets sharpened by brief grinding on the wheel.

The responsibility for the fact that the art of glass did not develop its full potentialities in England must be laid squarely to the door of the tax-gatherer. In 1745 a vicious tax, imposed on the weight of materials in the crucible, was levied on English glass. Despite the fact that a similar tax at the end of the seventeenth century had been abandoned because it damaged the industry and was difficult and troublesome to collect, the tax of 1745 was allowed to hamper development for nearly a century. The method of assessing the tax resulted in a reduction in the amount of lead, the heaviest ingredient, and consequently in the lustre and quality of the metal. Excessive decoration, in the form of shallow-cutting and engraving, was undertaken to offset the effect of this lack of quality.

The manner in which the tax was collected makes it surprising that anyone thought it worth while remaining in the industry, as witness the following extract from the evidence of a manufacturer before the Commissioner of Excise in 1833:

> Our business and premises are placed under the arbitrary control of a class of men to whose will and caprice it is most irksome to have to submit, and this under a system of regulations most ungracious and inquisitorial. We cannot enter parts of our own premises without their permission; we can do no one single act in the conduct of our business without having previously notified our intention to the officers placed over us.

It is not surprising that clandestine factories sprang up and disappeared making inferior glass from local materials until they attracted the notice of the Commissioners. Both masters and men combined to plague the Excise officer, who was the butt of all kinds of practical jokes and the victim of minor accidents with molten glass. The tax was not imposed in Ireland until 1825, but its pernicious effect in England may be judged from the rapidity with which the Irish industry declined thereafter.

Midway between domestic glass and that intended for

125 *God Appearing to Jonah*, painting on opaque white glass in the manner of engravings by J. W. Baur of Augsburg. Probably Nürnberg. *c.* 1710

126 An unusual cut-glass teapot. English. *c.* 1780

the luxury market came the products of Bristol, one of the centres for the manufacture of the popular blue glass for table use. Here, at the Redcliff Backs Glass-house, white opaque glass (which was undoubtedly produced in competition with imported and English-made porcelain) was enamelled in the porcelain style, the best often attributed to Michael Edkins, who, about 1760, is thought to have painted both delft and glass with the popular Chinese subjects [figure 139], and flowers and birds. Of better quality is the work of an English family of decorators, William and Mary Beilby (brother and sister), who worked on Newcastle glass, usually wine-glasses and decanters, from about 1762 until the middle of the 1770s. They employed a variety of *motifs*, and their work owes far less to contemporary porcelain fashions than did that of Edkins [figure 128]. Decoration in oil-gilding appears on both blue and white glass from Bristol and elsewhere, and the small *étuis* and scent-flasks, popular with the porcelain factories, also came from the glass-makers of Bristol and Staffordshire [figure 138].

127 A fine French moulded reproduction of cut-glass, the fluting to be compared with that of the decanter opposite. Nineteenth century

A popular type of coloured decorative glass was made at Nailsea, near Bristol, from 1788 until 1873, especially small items in which coloured glasses were spotted, intermingled, and juxtaposed in bold and swirling stripes, often with trailed threads in a *latticino* technique. These products include flasks, rolling-pins (sometimes said to be spirit-containers for smugglers), paper-weights, door-stops, pipes, walking-sticks, and a variety of small objects made at the lamp. Similar coloured and decorated glass was made at Sunderland and elsewhere.

Although Irish glass is much sought by collectors there is little difference between this and contemporary English work. In 1785 one of the Stourbridge manufacturers, John Hill, transferred his business and workmen to Waterford, and there made chandeliers and candelabra of all kinds, as well as boat-shaped bowls, those with a turned-over edge, complete dessert services, jugs, and drinking-vessels, all finely and deeply cut. The Irish glass-makers were not troubled by considerations of weight, and their glass could, therefore, be much thicker. The tax structure in England pressed glass dates from about 1840, although the greatest production was reached in the 1870s. Lacy glass is a variety of pressed glass introduced about 1829. The patterns are often based on revived rococo ornament popular at the time in Europe and America, with finely stippled backgrounds to the ornament produced by pressing.

It is impossible in so small a space to attempt to describe the enormous variety of coloured glasses made at this time, but towards the end of the nineteenth century many new kinds were developed, including imitations of hard-stones and those with an iridescent surface. Best known of this interesting group is the glass of Louis Tiffany of New York, whose speciality was 'favrile' glass [figure 134]. 'Favrile' — a trade name — was much influenced by *art nouveau*, the contemporary European style, and by the French maker of decorative glass, Emile Gallé. It is noted for its iridescent effects, probably suggested by the iridescence of excavated specimens.

In the twentieth century much important work has been done by the Steuben Glass Company. They have revived engraving and enamelling with notable success, and an example of Steuben engraving by Sydney Waugh is reproduced in figure 131.

128 Bottle (the base missing) enamelled with the Arms and Motto of the City of Newcastle inscribed 'Beilby Junr. pinxit and invt, N'Castle 1762'. On the reverse, the Arms of Sir Edward Blackett.

130 *(above)* Dessert dish on stand with scalloped rim and facet cutting of fine quality. The foot is moulded. Irish. Late eighteenth century

129 *(above left)* Jug of Nailsea glass, yellowish-green metal striped with white. English. *c.* 1800

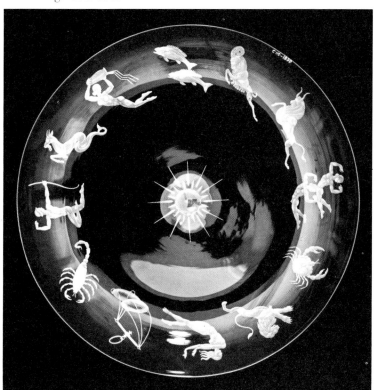

131 *(above)* Glass bowl, wheel-engraved with the signs of the Zodiac by Sydney Waugh. Steuben Glass Company. *c.* 1935

132 *(left)* English decanter of cut-glass, the vertical flutes at the base also cut. *c.* 1820

133 Press-moulded dish of opalescent glass. Eastern States of America. *c.* 1825

134 Decanter of 'favrile' glass. Engraved mark *LCT* for Louis C. Tiffany. Tiffany Glass and Decorating Company. New York. 1902

was such that duty was payable also on glass which was cut away, instead of on the finished object.

The industry hardly survived the extension of the tax to Ireland in 1825, and workers, technical knowledge, and capital were English in almost every case, especially at Waterford. There were glass-houses at Cork and Dublin. Cork specialized in rummers and decanters, and Dublin in chandeliers, bowls, decanters, and *épergnes.*

The production of glass in America is as old as the first European settlers. A glass-house was established at Jamestown, Virginia, in 1607. Early American glass was influenced more often than not by German glass, and more rarely by English. Little of what was made before 1800 now survives, but the glass of Henry William Stiegel (1729–1785), who came from Cologne to found a glass-house at Mannheim in Pennsylvania which worked between 1763 and 1774, is much sought, even though certain identification is rarely possible. Most of Stiegel's production seems to have been devoted to glass blown into moulds and decorated with enamelling and engraving. Caspar Wistar made glass in Salem County, New York, but his factory ceased to operate about 1780 and its products cannot be precisely identified. John Frederick Amelung from Bremen established a large glass-house at New Bremen, near Frederick in Maryland, which worked from 1785 to 1795 in the German tradition. Examples are now rare. His bankruptcy in 1795 released about five hundred skilled workmen who went elsewhere, principally to make utilitarian glass for which there was an ever-growing demand.

Mostly of unknown origin are the pictorial flasks popular among American collectors of early glass, of which there is a large and remarkable collection in the Corning Museum of Glass. These, transparent or coloured, belong to the first half of the nineteenth century, and the subjects are principally commemorative of contemporary events, Masonic symbols, and portraits.

The particular American genius for large-scale production began to show itself in the early years of the nineteenth century when glass blown or pressed into moulds, largely based on European cut-glass, was produced in large quantities. Immense amounts were made at Pittsburgh between 1848 and 1872, but the origin of the techniques is often attributed to a factory at Sandwich, Massachusetts, starting about 1827. This is very doubtful, although large quantities of pressed glass were made here. In matching sets

The art of glass

THE PRECEDING PAGES have been largely concerned with the historical aspects of glass. To discuss the value of glass as decoration is to move on to more difficult ground, especially at the present time when old values are being recklessly discarded in favour of a cult of amateurism in the arts generally. Glass-makers have always been craftsmen of a high order whatever technique they have adopted, and the lover of glass may, perhaps, console himself with the knowledge that he has four thousand years of tradition

135 *Verre églomisé*. The Penitence of St Mary Magdalene. Spanish. Seventeenth century

136 Decanter with gilt decorations, strongly reminiscent of painting on Chelsea and Worcester porcelain, from the studio of James Giles in Clerkenwell. *c.* 1765

in his favour, whereas the modern cult has been in existence for barely a couple of decades. If, in these remarks, I seem to lay unwonted stress on craftsmanship rather than on art, it is because this is something we can all recognize with a little experience; the second is all too often the plaything of passing fancies, and of ideas imposed, especially in these days, by insidious propaganda.

The manufacture of decorative glass is one of the few industries where the craftsman is still important. It is true that most domestic glass is now made in factories, blown automatically into moulds with all which this implies, but, with a few exceptions, this kind of work is not worth consideration. For the remainder the old processes, with a few modifications, still continue to be the principal methods of manufacture, and the lover of glass could hardly do better than try to see a factory of this kind in operation. It is the quickest and easiest way of acquiring knowledge essential to the connoisseur.

The decline in esteem which has affected most articles

157 Fountain of wrought and spur glass. Mid-nineteenth century. A good example of Victorian misapplied ingenuity

138 Scent-bottle and small box decorated with gilding. Similar small objects were fashionable in porcelain and enamel. Bristol. *c.* 1780

made by the true craftsmen stems largely from the application of the factory system to work of this kind during the nineteenth century, when the emerging *bourgeoisie* demanded showy objects as status symbols. Especially after the Great Exhibition of 1851 manufacturers increasingly adopted the essentials of most of the styles of the past, particularly those which could be adapted to semi-automatic and production-line methods. These *motifs* were blended with a happy disregard of the historical verities for an undiscriminating public. Here and there makers of decorative glass, such as Gallé and Lalique in France, and designers such as William Morris in England, ploughed a lonely furrow in attempts to make designs expressive of the true spirit of their time, or of a return to the more solid virtues of earlier craftsmanship, but they were exceptional then, and their followers have remained exceptional to this day.

It has been contended with a certain amount of truth that glass as an art did not reach a truly independent status until the invention of blowing, because only in this way did it become possible to exploit the peculiar properties of the material. Nevertheless, glass has probably been more valued at all times for its property of gathering and refracting light than for its plastic qualities, and engraving and cutting are more effective for this purpose than form alone. Glass-painting has always been related to the enamelling of metal and to the decoration of pottery.

The way in which old glass must be regarded is essentially dichotomous. The division between *diatretarii* and *vitrearii*, between decoration ultimately derived from hardstone carving (especially rock-crystal) and the plastic forms of blown glass, between the soda-glass traditions on the one hand and that of potash-glass (or lead-glass) on the other, will always remain. To a large extent these divisions have had a more profound effect on the style of glass than the more conventional styles in ornament. There is, for instance, no such classification into baroque, rococo, and neoclassical possible as may be made in the fields of pottery and metalwork, although a division into domestic and decorative glass can be made at all periods.

The art of glass is essentially western. Although the east has contributed some remarkably fine specimens of the glass-maker's skill, these have, for the most part, been derivative and isolated. Most Chinese glass, for instance, owes much to the jade-carver. Although glass was discovered in the Near East it was developed by European craftsmen after the first century AD, perhaps with the assistance of migrant Jewish workers, and it has remained predominantly a western craft ever since. Unlike pottery, metalwork, and furniture, signs of oriental influence, particularly Chinese, are very few.

139 (*above*) Characteristic vase of Bristol white glass based on a common porcelain form, painted in the manner of Michael Edkins. English.

140 (*left*) *The Last Judgement*. Scene constructed from glass made 'at the lamp'. Probably French (Nevers). Seventeenth century

The revival of the art in the twentieth century in Scandinavia is a little surprising because in the eighteenth century Swedish glass especially was hardly more than a provincial off-shoot of German, and there is no tradition of glass-making. Nevertheless, Swedish and Finnish manufacturers have produced some of the most distinguished work of this century. Excellent engraving has been done by the Steuben Glass Division of the American Corning Glass Company, and English glass-makers continue to produce well-designed domestic and industrial glass. The utilitarian requirements of the chemical industry have produced some singularly graceful forms.

Some remarks have already been made on the subject of forgeries. These will always be with us, and the new collector would do well to confine his acquisitions to glass from reliable sources until he has served his novitiate.

141 Glass fountain. The Great Exhibition. This 'far-famed crystal fountain is the gem of the transept, and has now a European celebrity. It contains four tons of pure colourless glass, it is twenty-seven feet high, and it might without difficulty be converted into a superb candelabrum, for which purpose its elegant design is eminently calculated.' *The Illustrated Exhibitor*, 1851